(continued)

Developmentally Appropriate Practice in "Real Life"

STORIES OF TEACHER PRACTICAL KNOWLEDGE

Carol Anne Wien

Foreword by Elizabeth Jones

TEACHERS
COLLEGE
PRESS

Teachers College · Columbia University
New York and London

for Sue Wolstenholme
with gratitude
for decades of commitment to
quality early childhood education

Published by Teachers College Press, 1234 Amsterdam Avenue, New York, NY
10027

Library of Congress Cataloging-in-Publication Data

Wien, Carol Anne.
    Developmentally appropriate practice in "real life" : stories of
teacher practical knowledge / Carol Anne Wien ; foreword by
Elizabeth Jones.
        p.   cm. — (Early childhood education series)
    Includes bibliographical references (p.   ) and index.
    ISBN 0-8077-3443-8 (alk. paper). — ISBN 0-8077-3442-X (pbk. :
alk. paper)
    1. Early childhood teachers — United States.   2. Early childhood
education — United States.   I. Title.   II. Series.
LB1775.2.W44   1995
72.21 — dc20   95-1838

ISBN 0-8077-3442-X (paper)
ISBN 0-8077-3443-8 (cloth)

Printed on acid-free paper

Manufactured in the United States of America

02 01 00 99 98 97 96 95   8 7 6 5 4 3 2 1

Contents

Foreword

In this stimulating book Carol Anne Wien welcomes the reader to the real world of teaching as experienced by five child-care teachers. It is clear that each teacher is doing her best for children. It is equally clear how difficult it can be to make practice developmentally appropriate, even when a teacher thinks she would like to; things-as-they-are keep getting in the way of things-as-they-might-be.

In any setting where one or a few adults work with large numbers of children, crowd control becomes the first priority. Most traditional practice for controlling children does not match the developmentally appropriate vision; it is less complex and more straightforwardly authoritarian. Further, most traditional practice for educating children derives from a view of academics as information learned by sitting still and listening; the good teacher keeps to the schedule and covers the lesson content. Child care has inherited the legacy of schooling.

Child-care teachers bring to their work the habits of response to children they have learned throughout their own long experiences of being parented and schooled, most often in an adult-dominated model. They also bring a healthy instinct for survival on the job. Survival always implies, when one is a newcomer in the setting, a conservative response of adapting to things as they are. Once habituated, relatively few teachers initiate significant changes in their practice.

We gain power to make changes in our lives as we learn to name our experiences. All of us need help in the naming process; language is a collective construction, and meaning emerges out of dialogue. Naming increases the possibility of control over our lives, as we review our experiences in the light of our values and discover whether our reality matches our ideal. We make changes when we experience the moral pain of conscious acknowledgment that things are not as we want them to be. In this process the role of the educator, mentor, pastor, therapist, researcher is to invite us to name the discrepancies and examine new possibilities for action. Wien's final interviews, she tells us, showed her "the pain of wanting to be constructing valued practice and not fully grasping what is meant by that." Moral pain is a fruitful source of energy for change. Collaborative talk about the details of practice makes possible the construction of meaning in action.

Often, of course, no one encourages us to retell or rethink our experience. Those in charge, whoever they are, prefer that practice remain as it is. Examination of the way things are is likely to lead to change, and change is a nuisance, an adventure into the unknown. "We don't want any adventures here, thank you!" says the hobbit Bilbo Baggins. "Nasty disturbing uncomfortable things! Make you late for dinner! I can't think what anybody sees in them." (J. R. R. Tolkien, *The Hobbit*, London: Allen & Unwin, 1937)

But Wien sees a lot in them, and she invites us to adventure with her through her retelling of teachers' stories. Storytelling puts practice in perspective and invites reflection and dialogue. Teachers need to read and hear others' stories and grow in the capacity to tell their own, assisted by nonjudgmental observers who can get the storytelling started.

Wien is one such observer. After observing, videotaping, and writing up her notes, she invited each teacher to join her in reflection on the observations. This is what I saw, she said in effect. Is it accurate from your perspective? Does it please you? If not, how might you go about changing it? In this approach, usable by supervisors and educators as well as researchers, teachers' strengths are acknowledged and their capacity for reflection on practice is nurtured. As a developmentally appropriate vision of work with teachers, it also models for teachers the elements of a developmentally appropriate approach to their work with children.

More directive supervision limits teachers' power to choose; and, as Wien makes clear, the critical difference between frameworks for action in early childhood education lies in the allocation of power. Young children in care are largely powerless unless teachers decide to share their power. Teacher dominion reflects the practice of most adults with children, spoken or implicit: do what I say because I say so and I'm the grownup. That is, of course, a valid rationale in some situations. But if we are to raise children with the capacity to care for self and others, to think critically and to make healthy choices in a society too full of destructive choices, we must nurture young children's initiative. Early childhood is the developmental stage meant for the exercise of initiative—choice-making—by children in the company of reliable adults: adults who value self-discovery and are willing to explore the whys of things. That assumption underlies developmentally appropriate practice. And, as Wien has documented, it is difficult to implement for most adults working with groups of young children.

The traditional practice called *teacher dominion* in this book aims for obedience, conformity, and the reduction of differences. In contrast, *developmentally appropriate practice* celebrates and tries to be responsive to differences—age/stage differences, individual differences, cultural differences (Mallory & New, 1994). To be responsive to differences requires greater attentiveness on the teacher's part and more flexibility of thought and action—more work, in short. Child care is already a lot of work; why make it harder?

Because, in an era in which, increasingly, young children are being cared for by strangers—people with no permanent personal commitment to them—competent professionalism looks like our primary hope for genuine caring for each child in group care. Professionalism is defined by reflection on practice. To reflect, we must tell our stories and give names to our experience, names that connect it with the values we hold and the theories that inform our work. Carol Anne Wien is a master storyteller. This book is a valuable resource for generating discussion of practice and the telling of many more stories.

Elizabeth Jones

Preface

This is a book about the work of five early childhood teachers, each in a different day care center, in an urban area with a population of several hundred thousand citizens. It is based on qualitative research — observations and fieldnotes, interviews and transcripts, videotaping and review with teachers — carried out in settings not connected with university education or lab schools. It does not set out to describe exemplary practice, although at times you will find this, nor to suggest what teachers should do, but to describe the practice of several teachers as it was found to be. It is a "slice of real life": the world it opens is that of the early childhood educator who has 7 hours of daily contact with children and none of the trimmings that accrue from proximity to education facilities or in-house lab settings. We see, in part, the grittiness of daily living with young children.

The original study grew out of a conflict that I felt as a teacher educator: why, after working with students to support their construction of the complex notions and performance skills necessary to provide developmentally appropriate practice for young children, and after seeing them become competent and full of vigor while in student practica, was it so seldom the case that developmentally appropriate practice appeared full blown in settings in the field? My impression was that student teachers of excellence would, within 2 or 3 years of entering work situations, be carrying out the commonplace patterns that make early childhood education in our area often look like traditional school trimmed down for size.

In studying five examples of teaching over the course of a year, and taking the next year to write about it, I developed four arguments that helped explain why developmentally appropriate practice is difficult to construct in early childhood settings. These arguments are mentioned in Chapter 1. However, for this book, I have lifted out from the complex relations that form teachers' daily work one contradiction in practice to examine, for I discovered that some teachers have an allegiance not to a single framework for practice but simultaneously to two contradictory frameworks. I have termed these contrasting frameworks *developmentally appropriate practice* and *teacher dominion*. Because both these frameworks are deeply embedded in the traditions of our society, teachers must of necessity negotiate their way through both forms of practice, coming to grips with them as they decide from moment to moment the best response that meets the immediate demand for action. Their pattern of doing so may be deeply entrenched in past actions in the setting, which they carry forward as inherited scripts for action, or they may stop and reflect, surface an action as problematic or inadequate, and generate something new.

What this book shows is five different examples of this negotiation process and how individuals, situated in their own complex and rich personal histories, choose to act. We see Jill, who seems balanced between the two frameworks, shifting from one to the other in moments of practice; Sonia, who wants to be more child-centered but discovers she is highly programmatic; Nora, who is shifting her values from one framework to another (unknown to either of us) even as we talked; Carla, who says her practice favors one framework when I thought it favored another; and Liz, who has a clear allegiance to a single framework and sets out to match her practice to her interpretation of this ideal. All names of teachers and children in the book are pseudonyms. Since there were no male teachers in my study, I use "she" when referring to teachers. I use either "he" or "she" for individual children, favoring "he" when "she" could be confused with the female teacher.

My hope is that readers who are early childhood teachers will see moments of practice like and unlike their own, will compare their own responses to moments described here, and will find a way to open up their own practice at the points where it is most troublesome to them, through the sort of reflection and generation of ideas that emerge from the persistent mulling over of an issue. I also hope the book illustrates — for teacher educators, administrators, consultants, supervisors, and all those who enter the arenas of early childhood but who do not work day by day with children — how the press of constraints and expectations and past habits can work against the construction of practice valued and intended by the teacher. It is surely our responsibility, too, whether we are in the classroom or not.

THE PARTICIPANTS AND THE SETTING

The city in which the teachers worked serves as the center for the region, offering the principal medical, educational, governmental, and cultural facilities for a geographic locale that is out of the mainstream and has always been economically troubled. The region's glaciated landscape of rock and evergreen, its harsh climate much of the year, its sparse population, and its economic underdevelopment lend particular poignancy to its culture, a culture of the underdog, of an area not much noticed. The city serving this region is more cosmopolitan than this suggests, attracting outside professionals, and is impressive enough in hills and water to seem, on a blue-sky day, like a young cousin to San Francisco.

The five centers in which the teachers worked were all in the downtown area of the city. Two settings were close to one of several local universities and drew on student, faculty, and professional families in the area. Another center was in a high school, with a mixed population of families (student, welfare, and professional), and two were in areas serving families in difficult economic circumstances, where unemployment and welfare were common. All the centers were established in the late 1960s and early 1970s and thus have long histories of established practice. Although the centers ranged in size from 63 to 380 children, they all serve families that are linguistically and racially diverse. Languages spoken, other than English, included French, Chinese, Vietnamese, Arabic, and Mi'kmaq. Black Canadian children were part of every center, both as recent immigrants and children of foreign students and as members of a local population that has been part of the city surround from its early days.

I have watched the centers develop for over 20 years, as a teacher educator, a researcher, and, in the early days, as an early childhood educator. The directors of these centers were enthusiastic about this project, because they saw it as speaking to an important issue—that of providing quality care for young children. Since I did not wish to work with teachers who knew me, or necessarily with the "stars" that come to directors' minds as ideal candidates for research, I asked the center directors for a pool of names from which I would randomly choose teachers to approach. We excluded from the pool of names teachers in their first year of work or under additional stress, such as pregnancy. With over 20 teachers suggested, I drew names from a hat and invited teachers individually to join the project. Some said no, they didn't want an observer exploring their work: they didn't like the idea of videotaping their program, or they were shy and thought someone else would do better, or they found administrative duties made the time commitment unworkable. I approached 11 teachers in order to gather up 5 participants. The teachers in this book, then, all had sufficient confidence, curiosity, and verve to open their work to an outsider and the professional courage to explore what we found together: in this sense, they were risk-takers.

I visited each teacher five or six times over several months. A visit included an observation of 1 to 3 hours during which I took fieldnotes, an interview of an hour or more after this observation, and, in all but the introductory visit, a videotaped portion (20 to 30 minutes) of her program. We reviewed the video during the interview, looking at what she expected would happen and comparing her hopes with what she saw. This process revealed both what she wanted to happen and her perception of what did happen. After this 5-month process, I reviewed my 750 pages of transcripts and fieldnotes and prepared a feedback paper for each teacher, synthesizing from her data set what I thought best presented her practical knowledge. Each of these required 2 weeks to write, so that the final interview occurred several months after the first cycle of visits.

We met for a long, intense final interview at which each teacher read the paper I had prepared for her and wrote comments in response. We then discussed these at length, as well as a criteria of 19 items representing aspects of developmentally appropriate practice that I had prepared out of the interaction of my observations in the field and the initial statement of developmentally appropriate practice (Bredekamp, 1987). I wanted to know whether each teacher saw herself as using aspects of this practice and how she valued it. Writing these feedback papers was an arduous process, but I wanted the teachers to have an opportunity to respond to what I saw in their work, both to keep the work authentic and to deepen my understanding. The teacher who disagreed with my portrayal prompted me to review the analysis and probe further to resolve this, a process that required 2 more months of analysis.

Finally, out of the feedback papers and the interview transcripts from the final interviews (another 250 pages of data), I built up the four arguments that I presented in my dissertation illuminating what makes it so difficult for teachers to construct developmentally appropriate practice, even when they appear to value it in their talk. The key to this sort of analysis is that any argument is checked against the entire data set concerned, both for material that confirms it and for material that does not (Erickson, 1986): if I found as much disconfirming as confirming evidence, I knew something else was going on, and I had not gotten to the bottom of it yet. But such "errors" themselves lead to sharper articulations, and this was how the arguments were constructed.

THE STRUCTURE OF THE BOOK

The book is organized in three sections—an introductory chapter, five case study chapters, and three chapters addressing issues common to all teachers, using material from these participants as examples. The introductory chapter describes the two central frameworks under consideration—teacher dominion and developmental appropriateness—and provides conceptual background on the concept of teacher practical knowledge. I discuss two essential processes in the formation of teacher practical knowledge: scripts for action and reflection-in/on-action in daily work. Each of the next five chapters offers the story of one teacher, with regard to the two frameworks under discussion. The conventions regarding citation of material from the data are as follows: within the brackets [ ] the name of the data set is specified by the teacher's initial. The first digit refers to the number of the visit and the second to the page number of the interview transcript; so, for example, [J3.21] refers to Jill's data set, third interview, page 21 of the transcript. Occasionally the reference indicates a source other than the interview transcripts: "F" refers to something described in fieldnotes; "V" means it is recorded on videotape; "per," as in [Jper20], refers to comments Jill made on page 20 of the feedback paper, and [Jwc] refers to written comments Jill provided on one occasion (at my suggestion) when she found several questions difficult to respond to orally.

Chapter 7 outlines six features of developmentally appropriate practice that were unfamiliar, in differing degrees, to several of the teachers, and indicates what they thought of them. In Chapter 8 I discuss scripts for action in teaching and how reflection-in/on-action breaks these open, with examples of each: watch for Liz's problem with toddlers unable to stop themselves from trucking sand up to housekeeping in the loft. The final chapter discusses criticisms of developmentally appropriate practice and sets the frameworks and teachers' negotiations of these in the notion of private and public domains of experience.

Lest there be any shade of doubt, I must own from the outset my obvious bias in favor of teacher construction of developmentally appropriate practice. This book is about enabling this practice to develop. At the same time, I acknowledge how steeped most of us are in processes of teacher dominion, out of our own frequent experience of schooling. As Britzman (1991) has pointed out, dualisms privilege one thing over another. In order to move beyond this, it is helpful to see teaching as a dialogic relation in which the teacher negotiates her way among myriad conflicting demands and processes, negotiating her own identity as teacher as she acts. This too, I hope you will see as you read.

ACKNOWLEDGMENTS

I have boundless admiration and respect for the teachers who opened their work to me, and for their directors, because it took courage and a vision of the contribution that research can make to the understanding of others. The children, as usual, make any endeavor in their presence a delight. But it is their teachers who have won my devotion. I thank them "with big heart," for there are times when it is not easy to see one's situation laid bare on the page, and this can only be done with the recognition that each teacher, each director, each center does everything in its power to provide well for the children in its care and wants the best for them.

Ann Manicom for years has helped me to set teacher practice in a more complex social context, and Kim Kienapple asked the sort of questions that push one's thinking forward. Joseph Murphy quite simply made the original study possible through his confidence in my work and through the harmonious work relationships he establishes around him. These three were my committee members for my dissertation, and their contribution to my work is immeasurable. Catherine Krupnick, through her class on improving teaching at the Harvard Graduate School of Education in 1989, sparked my excitement for the potential of video as a tool in consulting with teachers and opened up a new set of possibilities for encountering a teacher's work. I thank, too, Deborah Britzman for recent colleagial conversations that stir the mind.

Carol Copple and Elizabeth Jones offered enthusiasm and interesting comments that have had their impact on this work, and I thank them. Susan Liddicoat has provided impeccable comments and editing that have served to strengthen the book: it is a blessing to work under an eye both sharp and meticulous. And I am grateful for Peter Sieger's exquisite clarity and cheery voice in guiding me through several computer problems.

My husband, Fred Wien, knows the role in my life of his extraordinary equilibrium as both anchor and harbor of safety, and this book would not have been possible without his technical help with computers, which render me in need of that equilibrium.

1 Teachers' Work in Early Childhood

Early childhood educators across North America are caught in a conflict embedded in our society: is teacher dominion or developmental appropriateness the best route to learning and development for young children? A teacher who one moment corrects a child who is crushing tissue shapes in his fist because she wants him to see their geometric shapes, and who later suggests to another child — also crumpling them into bits — that "sometimes they look nice that way" is acting in each case in a way consistent with a particular frame of reference for the education of young children. In the first instance, she instructs, corrects, and shapes children's responses to her purposes, an instance of teacher dominion. In the second, she permits the child's intention to shape his own activity and supports this by acknowledging it, an instance of developmental appropriateness. This book explores how both these frameworks for professional practice can be present in the work processes of individual teachers.

In the broader community of early childhood education — in the arenas of academic research, publishing, teacher training, accreditation of programs — these contrasting frameworks for teacher action, each with its own theoretical underpinning and passionate adherents, may seem to teachers to be like separate camps tussling over disputed territory. Unquestionably there is real struggle about what it is best to do for young children. Teacher educators tend to regard the frameworks as incompatible (because they are theoretically mutually exclusive), and as individuals we favor one over the other as a consequence of our own rich and complex personal history.

However, in the work of teachers in early childhood, these two contrasting frameworks for action are often intertwined with unconscious intimacy in the day-to-day processes of individual teachers. Practice is a struggle to prioritize cherished values, and it may be rare to find in one individual a set of ideals closely matching a single "overarching theory" of practice [the phrase is Donald Schön's (1983)], for lived life is more dynamic, conflicted, muddied. However, we will see in this book one teacher with a clear allegiance to one framework for action. We will also see four teachers whose practice displayed, in differing degrees and levels of

1

awareness, an allegiance to both teacher dominion and developmental appropriateness.

I began the research project that formed the foundation for this book as a teacher educator. I started with the conflict I felt between what I had tried for years and years to enable early childhood educators to do and the contrasting reality I saw before me when I supervised in the field. I held an ideal image based on my experience, training, and interpretation of the ideology of developmentally appropriate practice, an ideology that links many members of the early childhood community in North America. However, in the field I could frequently see that carrying out this practice was very difficult for teachers. Rather than providing situations where children could engage in child-initiated activity, play freely with friends, and try out absorbing activities in an atmosphere of exploration and a climate of social responsibility (as the ideology suggests), day care centers more frequently operated like miniature factories, with fixed time periods for activities and children moving through them as if they were in an assembly line: 9:30 was snack time, no matter how absorbed Susan and Graham might have become in making fingerpaint designs. Initially, I puzzled over what made it so difficult, in day care centers in particular, for teachers to construct developmentally appropriate practice. I found that individual teachers tolerated allegiances to conflicting sets of practices, swinging from one to the other, and that systemic constraints external to teachers as well as some unfamiliarity with developmental appropriateness interacted with these. Although each teacher's practice was unique in certain respects, her own story at a specific moment in time, there are shared elements which apply beyond individuals and illuminate the practice of others.

In this first chapter I wish to make clear the context that surrounds any teacher's work in early childhood. There are three threads to hold in mind. One is the teacher herself, the totality of personality and rich background experience encapsulated in her presence at any given moment. The second thread is the two specific frameworks for practice under discussion — teacher dominion and developmental appropriateness — which we disentangle in order to talk about, but which are intertwined in our work lives, even if we reject one. The third thread is the concept of teacher practical knowledge and how it is embedded in teacher actions and talk about those actions. This book displays aspects of the practical knowledge of five day care teachers and shows how the two broader frameworks are interpreted and become part of teacher action in each case. We will look at the two contrasting frameworks for action, and then I will outline the concept of practical knowledge as I am using it, to construct the common ground we share as readers for the work that follows.

TWO FRAMEWORKS: TEACHER DOMINION
AND DEVELOPMENTAL APPROPRIATENESS

When Carla sends children to the bathroom from circle, they line up at the door and wait for her to lead the line; a child who "wibbles" in line, bothering others, stays behind on the time-out chair. Sonia, in the same context, sings a song in the circle that sends three children at a time to the bathroom, staggering the group so some still sing as others wash up; there is no line-up and minimal waiting for facilities.

In Liz's room all the areas for play — housekeeping, sand, water, manipulative materials — are always available to the children, any time of day. In Nora's room one or two play areas, usually blocks or housekeeping, are "closed" about one-third of the play time and children ask permission to use them when they "open."

In Carla's "show-and-tell" circle, nine children are asked to think up a question for each child's object so that everyone has a turn. Waiting and verbal turn-taking occupy 40 minutes of sitting together quietly listening and talking. In Jill's "show-and-tell" five children briefly display and discuss their chosen objects and spend 20 minutes playing with them, exploring the Mickey Mouse doll, sending the slinky down the loft stairs, trying on the bead necklace.

In these contrasting examples we see different expectations for how young children and their teachers live together through the long days they share. But their expectations and practice are neither random nor haphazard, and much of what they do matches one or more frameworks of practice. The broad values, beliefs, attitudes, and feelings — the view of children and their relation to adults that is shared by a community — is sometimes called an ideology (Apple, 1979; Rokeach, 1968; Sharp & Green, 1975) or a discourse (Britzman, 1991; Lubeck, 1994), but here I prefer the term *framework*. I choose *framework* because it includes not only the beliefs and values held by a community, its world view, and the particular language in which this takes shape, but also the notion of the specific sets of practices necessary to encompass the discourse or ideology in lived life. The term *framework* combines theory and practice, and for teachers they are inseparable (Clandinin, 1986; Elbaz, 1983). The term *framework* is also more concrete, for it carries the image of an outline, a coherent structure, like the skeleton of 2 × 6s framing a house under construction, which can carry the weight of materials necessary to shelter a family in space and time. So a framework for practice, in its articulated outline, carries the weight of all the myriad practices, myths, beliefs, values, and feelings that accompany living with children in space and time. Ideology is sometimes seen as a blueprint for action [Sharp and Green (1975) critique this notion], but a framework is the very structure in practice that holds people's work together: ideology and discourse give it shared meaning.

There are many frameworks for practice in early childhood, and the more precisely they are detailed the more distinctive they become: think of Montessori, Waldorf, Suzuki, Reggio Emilia, Warner, A. S. Neill. However, within the mainstream of education there are two poles in frameworks for practice (with many programs at some intermediate position between them on a continuum toward the extremes) that appear to be present throughout the history of education in one form or another. Both poles include a number of differing frameworks for practice that nevertheless share a common core. They encompass different and contrasting world views, then, and Western society, with its democratic values favoring plurality, encourages competing views as a way to strengthen a flourishing culture. These two poles are teacher dominion and developmental appropriateness. This is not the place to set out a history of teacher-centered practice and developmentally appropriate practice: thus the following sections are intended to highlight the main differences between them and set them briefly in context.

The Location of Power Within Each Framework

The key difference between teacher dominion and developmental appropriateness is in the conception of the location of power. By power I mean the possibility of taking action in the world, of being an active agent, of having agency. Each framework imagines a different child and a different truth about the nature of children and their development. In teacher dominion, the location of power is in the adult. The child is viewed as a container—Locke's *tabula rasa*, or empty slate (1693/1964)—to be filled with knowledge: the adult transmits knowledge through direct instruction and the child accumulates desired knowledge like a jug filling with water (Crain, 1992). In developmental appropriateness, the location of power alternates between adult and children, with power shared. Both adults and children are believed to be active agents who seek out and construct knowledge through active interaction with others (Duckworth, 1987; Kamii & DeVries, 1978/1993; Piaget, 1937/1954). In teacher dominion, sources of knowledge about the world are located in the teacher. In developmental appropriateness, sources of knowledge are multiple, shared among those participating in a social world.

In both frameworks for practice, teachers use teacher direction — they teach — but the way instruction is used differs. In teacher dominion it is the principal mode by which learning is seen to occur, and the child is obligated to receive it. In developmental appropriateness it is but one of a variety of ways the child comes to understand his or her world: it is offered and the child is free to accept or reject it.

I use the term *teacher dominion*, rather than *teacher direction*, to describe one framework for action because teaching occurs in *both* practices and because the sense of dominion describes the location of power within the teacher. Teacher dominion asserts the teacher's authority in all domains except when she explicitly removes it, as in recess or "free play" (which means free from teacher instruction). Developmental appropriateness asserts that children should be permitted agency, the right to self-chosen action in a field, taking their age and individual needs and interests into account (Bredekamp, 1987). In teacher dominion the teacher expects to be in charge, to choose goals, plan and implement activities, and evaluate outcomes (Bereiter & Engelmann, 1966; Brophy & Good, 1986). In developmental appropriateness teachers are prepared to manage resources and organize children, to lead activity and set the agenda, and also to give up the lead, in part, to permit children to influence the flow of activity, to offer ideas, plans, and questions where they can take responsibility for these, and then to use what emerges from the children in order to lead again, to let go again (see, for instance, Hohmann, Banet, & Weikart, 1978; Jones & Nimmo, 1994; Jones & Reynolds, 1992; Katz & Chard, 1989; Paley, 1990). They differ, too, in how they view the teacher. Teacher dominion sees the teacher as a dispenser of knowledge that she has already mastered, whereas developmental appropriateness sees the teacher as a co-inquirer with children about the world (Edwards, Gandini, & Forman, 1993; Mallory & New, 1994). Each framework has a different view of how the child's right to education is fulfilled.

Historical Roots of the Frameworks

Both frameworks for practice have been present, in one form or another, as long as formal schooling has existed and can be traced, in their North American forms, back to the ideas of Locke (1693/1964) on the one hand and Rousseau (1764/1979) on the other. Locke's belief that experience is fundamental in forming the mind, as well as his empiricism, appealed to American educators of the nineteenth century, inspiring Mann's school reform (Power, 1991). There are many links between positivism (Comte,

1830–1842/1975), behaviorism and social learning theory (Bandura, 1969; Bandura & Walters, 1963), technical rationalism (Tyler, 1950/ 1968), and the industrial, factory-like model of schooling so familiar to many of us, where school time is fragmented like an assembly line into periods into which separate subject matter is slotted, like eggs in a crate. The child is taught via teacher-centered practice and viewed as a product to serve labor market demands (Apple, 1979; Giroux & Penna, 1981). The influence of positivism, behaviorism, and technical rationalism is reflected in school characteristics and values such as

> standardization, conformity, atomistic information, deductive logic, abstraction, linear/analytic knowledge (Hilliard, 1976), scientific ex- planations for everything, future-time orientation, working to get ahead, efficient use of time, climbing the ladder of success, competition, striving to win, individuality, and saving for the future (Shade, 1989). (C. B. Phillips, 1994, p.146)

Why does this matter when considering early childhood settings, which function largely outside the domain of formal schooling?

It matters because, for whatever reasons (and to my knowledge these have not yet been adequately researched) day care settings in particular, such as those represented in this book, frequently take as the structure of their day a traditional school format. That is to say, they function using a school-like time schedule for activities and routines, and much of the teacher's job is sustaining the routine. Children are separated by 1-year age groups into separate programs, like grades, and move up at the end of the year. Why the school was adopted as the model format for many early childhood settings is unclear, and it may well have happened unreflec- tively, simply because other possibilities were not obvious and school was a salient model for the social world of children and adults. However it occurred, this adoption of a traditional school format for holding together group life in day care has had profound consequences for how teachers work with young children, as these case studies will show: sometimes teachers hardly seemed aware of this aspect of their practice, it was so taken for granted as normal. Apple (1979) speaks of hegemony as a form of domination by a culture and describes it as a saturation of the conscious- ness such that the very things that seem most ordinary, most taken for granted, are in fact the dominating elements. They dominate the meaning and value we give to events. In early childhood settings the structuring of time like school is one of these.

Developmentally appropriate practice is much more self-conscious and consciously held by teachers, perhaps because it is still so new, only receiving its first clear and widely held articulation in 1987 (Bredekamp). But its cultural roots trace back to Rousseau's belief in the natural goodness of children (1764/1979) and the importance of personal goals (Crain, 1992), through the route of Froebel's kindergarten movement, the maturational and observational studies of children in the 1930s and 1940s (Gesell, 1940, 1948/1971), and on through the influence of Piaget's constructivism (Ginsburg & Opper, 1969; Piaget & Inhelder, 1969) and cognitive and ecological psychology (Bronfenbrenner, 1979; Bruner, 1986; Vygotsky, 1978).

Manifestations of the Frameworks for Practice

How is teacher dominion as a practice manifested in the world of early childhood education? It is reflected in specific programs, from the Bereiter–Engelmann models originated in the 1960s, through DISTAR, to the more recent conceptions of Madeleine Hunt, which focus on academic content taught via workbooks. But it is also manifested through a set of work conditions that are distinctly factory-like in process, whether dealing with academic worksheets or the structure of day care centers. Typically there is an industrial notion of time as scarce, with strictly kept time schedules and fixed purposes for activities that begin and end when the teacher specifies (often these are determined by events outside the classroom). There is a routine to be accomplished by the teacher that includes shepherding her group of children through basic needs such as toileting, eating, and napping. Conformity to teacher purposes in carrying out the routine is paramount.

Developmental appropriateness is in its youth, still adjusting to its moniker, still evolving but also suggesting that a dynamic model of practice will always evolve, responsive to varying conditions and times (Bredekamp & Rosegrant, 1992). This ideology is evidenced in the world in several ways. It takes the form of documents that have been widely accepted by member organizations of the early childhood community, formulated over a number of years via a broad consultation process (Caldwell, 1984) and ratified by memberships. These documents include position statements on developmentally appropriate practice (Bredekamp, 1987) and curricula (Bredekamp & Rosegrant, 1992), position statements on accreditation procedures for programs that implement developmentally appropriate practice (NAEYC, 1986a, 1986b), and mammoth research projects and literature reviews undertaken to examine various aspects of quality child care and make recommendations with regard to this practice (such as D. Phillips & Howes, 1987; Ruopp, Travers, Glantz, & Coelen, 1979; Whitebrook, Howes, & Phillips, 1990). It is evidenced in some training programs that attempt to educate teachers for early childhood and restrict their program to developmentally appropriate practice, rather than using an eclectic approach; High/Scope is one such program (Hohmann et al., 1978). It is evidenced in guidelines or mission statements adopted by particular organizations such as school boards and teacher professional associations. It is evidenced in individual teachers who construct for themselves an understanding of the ideology and attempt to practice it.

Characteristics of Teacher Dominion and Developmentally Appropriate Practice in This Study

Moving from this general context to the classrooms of the teachers in this book, there were five dimensions of activity used by the participants in this study that can be characterized as occurring in teacher-centered or developmentally appropriate ways. When practice followed teacher dominion, classroom activities bore the following characteristics.

1. The teacher chooses the activity, its purposes, and its design, and then implements it. Ownership of the activity belongs to the teacher: part of the activity is persuading children to her purposes, motivating them.
2. The teacher controls the agenda for action, that is, there is a prescribed range of possible responses that the children are permitted. Activity outside the range is corrected.
3. The activities are obligatory. Children are to do them in order to learn specific content.
4. The activities are generally conducted in large groups.
5. There is a fixed schedule of events, the routine, with the teacher moving from one activity to the next as she conducts the children through them.

Developmentally appropriate practice, in contrast, is described as holistic, focused on the individual, interactionist (Genishi, Dyson, & Fassler, 1994), and emphasizing respect (Wien, 1991). In developmental appropriateness, sources of knowledge about the world are multiple, the teacher but one of them, and the child is viewed as an active seeker, constructing understanding through mental and physical interactions with people and with materials. The child's activity, enlisting his or her whole person, mentally and physically, is seen as instrumental in forming an understanding about the world. The location of power about what to do is given back to the child: it is this point that can be easily misunderstood, for it does not mean the child can do anything she wishes. The teacher holds responsibility for the social welfare of her group, and the child's individual activity is limited by social responsibility to the group. But within this, there is broad toleration for the child's choice and pace in determining activity. When practice was developmentally appropriate, classroom activities bore the following characteristics.

1. The child chooses activity from a broad range of possibilities provided by the teacher, and both teacher and children contribute to the design and implementation of activities. Power over what to do is shared among children and adults, with the adult holding responsibility for the group.
2. Children control the agenda for their own activity where they are able to assert it. A broad range of constructive responses is tolerated by teachers.
3. Teachers provide a wide range of activities and materials, among which children may choose and with which they plan and carry out their intentions in many different ways.
4. Activities are in general individual or done in small groups.
5. Different activities occur simultaneously, with some children working individually, some with teachers, and a flexible schedule of events permitting spontaneous activity.

The basic belief system of each framework is in opposition to the other. Where developmental appropriateness argues that learning is child-centered and holistic, stating that children must be permitted to be active decision makers about their own activity, that they learn with their entire body and not simply the mind, teacher dominion is teacher-centered and fragments learning into components, placing an authority external to the learners in control of the pace, direction, and focus of learning. Where teacher dominion emphasizes mastery of specific content and frames action in terms of the group, developmental appropriateness emphasizes individual development and frames action in terms of a unique child. (Both frameworks value respect and goals.)

The two frameworks for practice, teacher dominion and developmental appropriateness, which are culturally shared among broad communities, are clearly separate from (but obviously have connections to) the personal theory or philosophy that each teacher constructs for herself. In the mental activity of the teacher, the contents of the frameworks as she experiences them interact with the totality of her personal history and temperament, and she appropriates an approximation of the frameworks through absorption and reflection as she lives them. Thus they become part of her, an interpretation of these discourses grounded in her lived experience. Her personal theory has unique aspects, personal to her, as well as features shared with others who also accept the frameworks. It is these shared features that make her a part of the broader community. As well, her personal theory can be considered separately from her practice, and yet her practice can never be separate for it is always informed by her theories-in-action.

THE PRACTICAL KNOWLEDGE OF TEACHERS

In examining the relation between thought and action in teaching, the traditional approach is to think of theory and practice and thus to pose them as a dualism. But this conventional stance separates them, like the two arms of a balance. It further results in an image of theoreticians somehow injecting theory into teachers, who assimilate it like an inoculation and then inject it into practice. And, just as this conception puts theory first (it would be unconventional to say "practice to theory"), so there is an implicit assumption that we start with theory, idea, abstract thought, in order to understand practice. But as Connelly and Clandinin (1986) remind us, we do not understand practice by beginning with theory but by studying practitioners and classrooms as they are. The heart of teaching is action, performance, and the penumbra of belief, attitude, feeling tone, sense of values, personality, and background experience of the teacher that surrounds and contributes to each lived moment of practice. The notion of practical knowledge includes all that the teacher brings of herself to the moment of teaching—beliefs, attitudes, feelings, reflection, gestures, temperament, personal history (Clandinin, 1991).

Performance is enabled by a combination of conscious know-how and tacit or hidden knowledge (Polanyi, 1958). One of the key things about tacit knowledge is that it is inarticulate, not easily surfaced or verbally expressed. A classic example provided by Polanyi is the recognition of faces. We do this unconsciously, easily remembering whether a face is new or not, although the name for a recognized face may well be forgotten, but to describe the process by which we recognize another's face is too difficult. Nor could I consciously describe how I improvise when I play the piano, or how I know what to do when I sight read and can suddenly "tell" how the piece is supposed to sound. It is too complex. Anything said would be but a fraction of what goes into action. The notion of the inseparability of theory and action, theory and practice, has long roots, but Polanyi's conception of tacit knowledge is the taproot for much work that followed.

Any action is informed not simply by conscious thought—that is but the tip of the iceberg—but also by tacitly understood processes of performance that underlie and structure it. The conscious aspect is underlaid in practice with all sorts of assumptions and taken-for-granted aspects. (And some actions are, of course, primarily automatic, based on tacit knowledge.)

Freema Elbaz (1983) was the first researcher with teachers, to my knowledge, who captured the inseparability of theory and practice for the practitioner in her conceptualization of practical knowledge. Her point was that theory is enacted in the actions of the teacher, that actions display both practice and the theory that informs them, and she showed this in the work of one high school teacher. Clandinin (1986) built upon her work by addressing the area of images in teacher practice. The image, which is a coalescence of theory and practice, acts as a gathering-up, a prescriptive quintessence of what the teacher attempts to do. [Schön (1983) describes the reflective practitioner as having an "overarching theory, an appreciative system" (p. 164) that gives the performance or practice coherence; this I see as very close to Clandinin's use of the term *image*.] Clandinin found five such images for one teacher, six for another, but the reader does not have the sense that these coalesced into a single coherent structure which each teacher could use, but that the images were separate, perhaps restricted to particular contexts. This left room for the possibility of conflict, of contradiction among them: what circumstances would call each into action?

It is the work of Berlak and Berlak (1981) that is particularly rich in portraying struggles, conflicts, and tensions in the work of teachers, in this instance, elementary school teachers in Britain. They focus their attention on "dilemmas" in the practice of teachers, describing 16 of these, in the realms of extent of control over the child, of what counts as knowledge, and of the relationship of the child to the society at large. They describe what is at the heart of teaching for the teacher—a continuous tussle with the self concerning what choice of action one should make, and a continual prioritizing of one choice over all the other possibilities for action.

Berlak and Berlak (1981) examined the teachers' struggles in terms of dominant and exceptional patterns of resolution of teacher dilemmas. For instance, one day Mr. Scott permitted Steven to play with his baseball cards rather than ask him to do math (an exceptional resolution), whereas the next day the same child was required to do an entire page or he would lose a privilege. For Berlak and Berlak, their concept of an act is derived from George Herbert Mead, who saw any action as informed by three aspects—the sense of the "me" as active agent who initiates action, the past actions of that agent, and the self as acted upon by society through the weight of past patterns of action. "The act is a process that includes its history and is continuous with its future" (p. 116).

Some actions are thus done automatically, as patterns given by society. Berlak and Berlak (1981), borrowing a term from psychology (where it carries a narrower meaning), refer to these as "habituated responses," as "dispositions to act . . . taken from past experience" (p. 114). Schutz's (1976) articulation of this same idea as "recipe" knowledge has perhaps had wider circulation. Again, his point too is that much that we take for granted as our personal knowledge is passed on to us by society, already formed, patterned: we take and use it. A 3-year-old accepts that an elephant lives in a zoo without direct experience of either. I think this is a powerful idea, but the term that I prefer as a descriptor for the taken-for-granted patterns of knowledge and consequent action is neither *habituated response* nor *recipe*, but *script*. We have scripts for action that originate outside us.

Scripts for Action in Practical Knowledge

Practical knowledge is a broad term that encompasses all a teacher does in her setting. One aspect of this is the scripted patterns of action she follows and her mental scripts for these. Berlak and Berlak (1981) noted, for instance, that sometimes teachers' resolutions to dilemmas were deliberate and "at other times teachers' patterns seemed almost totally mindless, sheer habit, or formed by cultural and social experiences and forces, or by internal needs of which they were but dimly or not at all aware" (p. 108). These are the tacit patterns, the taken-for-granted aspects of work processes, carried through automatically. Scripts for action are one type of theory-in-action, absorbed and carried out without conscious effort or thought.

The notion of a script for action is broad: it includes not simply conceptual information but feelings, perceptions, images of action, goals, and expectations interacting in space and time (Schank & Abelson, 1977). Mandler (1984) points out that it was Schank and Abelson who coined the term *script* "to characterize our knowledge of familiar event sequences" (p. 75). By this they mean our knowledge structures about common routines — such as going to MacDonald's or eating lunch at the day care center. Script theory attempts to describe mental representations of underlying structures in memory. Although I have adopted the term *script*, I use it to refer to repeated routines and how these are embedded in teacher actions. I use it in a straightforward way to refer to external action, not internal representation. Here *scripts for action* refers to repeated patterns of routine practice that teachers use. Much of daily life is lived easily, semiautomatically, because we know the script and find the situation highly predictable. For instance, as Nelson (1977) reminds us, much of the work of the very young child is finding predictable patterns in a novel world. The idea of script-based knowledge makes intuitive as well as theoretical sense in thinking about teaching and percolates through the literature, turning up in areas as disparate as curriculum theorizing (Halkes, 1988), explanations of children's play (Bretherton, 1984), and studies of literacy and language (Yawkey & Pellegrini, 1984). How might scripts for action function in early childhood settings?

Once a pattern of action works successfully to accomplish a teacher need, it is likely to be used again. It then quickly becomes an established pattern for accomplishing a task: if it works, it becomes automatic and frees the teacher to think of something else. Since there will always be multiple demands upon the attention of the teacher, some things must be done automatically so that she can attend to others. As an example, a day care teacher who always finishes her group circle with the song "One Elephant Went out to Play," repeating the song many times until all the children have gone off in small groups of four or five to the bathroom, clearly has an instrumental script for moving children through the transition from circle to bathroom. Her script for action allows each child to have a turn in the song, permits the children to be spaced out in time in using the bathroom, prevents the children from having to line up and wait, and allows those still waiting in circle to be active by singing the song. And its focus on permitting young children to be meaningfully active during a transition time marks it as developmentally appropriate. Used day after day, it becomes a permanent script for action, the transition from group activity to bathroom.

Scripts help to make action routine. Scripts are embedded with theory, too, but it is taken-for-granted theory, that is, tacit knowledge not easily articulated. The script-based knowledge that exists about early childhood work in teachers encapsulates (in part) how to put theory into practice, insofar as practice is bound by scripts. As activity becomes more creative, more reflective, and more conscious, it is less script-bound (or at least the scripts are subsumed). Nevertheless, theory is implicit in scripts for action as much as in the more reflective situations.

Clearly each framework for practice will have its own scripts, as reflections of this theory-in-action. A script for action presumes the comprehensive set of beliefs about the world from which it results. Developmentally appropriate practice produces different scripts than teacher dominion. But only part of practice is script-bound.

Reflection in Practical Knowledge

Reflection as an interactive tool by which theory and action become inseparable has received concerted attention in the past decade through the
efforts of Donald Schön (1983, 1987). He speaks of the "design-like art-
istry of professional practice" (1987, p. 158), and early childhood educators fit this definition of a profession as design-like work: "Herbert Simon
and others have suggested that all occupations engaged in converting actual to preferred situations are concerned with design" (1983, p. 77).

Schön (1983) argues that professional practice is reflection-in-action.
Professionals cope constantly with "awareness of uncertainty, complexity,
instability, uniqueness, and value conflict" (p. 17), all of which may result
in diverging views of what the particular practice should be. He argues
that the practitioner has an "overarching theory, an appreciative system"
(p. 164) that provides the sense of how things are supposed to be.

Schön (1983) argues that reflection-in-action arises out of a kind of
knowledge that is largely inarticulate and unconscious: "in much of the
spontaneous behavior of skillful practice we reveal a kind of knowing
which does not stem from a priori intellectual operation" (p. 50). He
describes reflection-in-action by practitioners as "on the spot surfacing,
criticizing, restructuring and testing of intuitive understandings of experienced phenomena" (p. 241). Part of it, too, is tacit.

> When someone reflects-in-action, he becomes a researcher in the prac-
> tice context. He is not dependent on the categories of established theory
> and technique, but constructs a new theory of the unique case. His
> inquiry is not limited to a deliberation about means which depends on a
> priori agreement about ends. He does not keep means and ends separate,
> but defines them interactively as he frames a problematic situation.
> (p. 68)

For Schön, then, the reflection-in-action, the thought displayed in acting
on the environment, is intuitive, complex, and artistic and arises out of a
totality of experience as a professional. How might this apply to the context of early childhood programs?

Here is an instance of reflection in which a mature student teacher
discovered an absorbing activity for a lively, dominant 4-year-old boy who
displayed a well-developed habit of annoying adults:

> The teacher notices that Jacob, who seldom chooses activity indoors,
> but prefers to wander, flitting from child to child, joking, poking,
> rolling his body around the backs of chairs, becomes absorbed out-

doors on the playground digging in the sand. He works at this con-
tentedly for up to 30 minutes, alone or with a pal. Inside he ignores
the sandbox. She decides the indoor sand is too dry, too shallow, and
too thinly spread, and creates, with Jacob in mind, a digging activity
using potting soil, garden trowels, and tools and several deep buckets
which permit the dirt to be moved around. Not only Jacob but several other children are absorbed by this and use it for several weeks.
(Notes from supervision of student teachers)

When the teacher creates this activity, she is using the totality of her
knowledge about child development, about what is good for children and
what will appeal to them, her understanding of this particular child [that
he is bored inside, not "hooked" (Hunt, 1964) into anything in the envi-
ronment], and her own resources and skills as a gardener to create something that will work for him at that moment. The problem she sets is how
to involve Jacob in activity indoors, and she arrives at a solution by her
critique of what is there (the unsatisfactory sandbox) and by restructuring
an outdoor activity for indoor use. In the process, she creates something
new for that child, for herself as a teacher, and for the classroom as a
whole. This both fits Schön's conception of reflection-in-action and illustrates the design aspect of early childhood education.

Perhaps Schön's concept of professional practice as reflection-in-
action describes the most productive moments of practice, when a solution
is generated or a new direction formulated. This is the creative aspect
of practice; it describes the high point, not the totality, of professional
practice.

As early childhood settings are currently organized, much practice is
not professional in Schön's sense of the term, but routinized menial tasks
of the most repetitive kind. Much of current day care practice concerns
the carrying out of mundane routines (bathroom duty, serving lunch,
arranging cots, fixing snacks, washing tables, changing diapers, or helping
children dress), and these quickly become automatic scripted actions.
Practice as reflection-in-action addresses that part of practice that concerns framing and solving a problem. If a day care teacher accepts her
situation unreflectively, then she will attempt neither to set nor to solve
small problems in the setting but will remain as a stable force of inertia
within the system. She will perpetuate the system in place, whatever it
may be, because of the particular way that humans understand repetitive,
predictable situations; they call up automatic scripts.

In considering the student teacher who made the gardening activity,
it is clear that reflection-in-action and reflection-on-action can only be
separated with difficulty, for the thinking and acting that occur around a

problem occupy more than the moments in action (Wien, 1991). They interweave over time. Let me clarify my sense of reflection-in-action and reflection-on-action. Reflection-in-action presumes thought during and embedded in action. Reflection-on-action presumes thought about action separate from the action itself. In one, thought is embedded in action, and in the other, in words. The advantage of reflection-on-action is that it can be more easily communicated, acknowledged, and shared with another. But this difference between them can lead us to regard them as separate, distinct aspects of human functioning, and I think this is incorrect, for both reflection-in-action and reflection-on-action have tacit and conscious aspects; the balance changes as one moves from action to thinking about action. It may be more fruitful to think of one occurring relatively spontaneously, in the heat of the moment, and the other having a longer life span, occurring over days or even months in a cycle of thought and action. Nor is it correct to think of one as mostly tacit and the other as primarily deliberate, as one might first be tempted. Both draw upon considerable tacit knowledge and both have deliberate components. Although other researchers separate them (Connelly & Clandinin, 1990; Yinger, 1986), I prefer to think of them as the same process used differently over time and I express this notion as reflection-in/on-action.

The Relation of Scripts for Action to Reflection-in/on-Action

My sense of practical knowledge is that two of the most essential processes by which the teacher functions are her scripts for action and her reflection-in/on-action. It is the dynamic interplay of these as a teacher interprets the frameworks for practice that she uses that can produce (or not produce) moments of change in her practice: it becomes fascinating to explore. Both processes are necessary if she is to function comfortably in a setting. Think of learning to drive, and how no attention can be paid to road conditions or other vehicles until the actions necessary to drive the car have become automatic.

Eisner (1985), too, notes how scripts are necessary in order to make change possible:

> It is through repertoires or routines that the teacher can devote his or her energies and attention to what is emerging in class. . . . It is precisely the tension between automaticity and inventiveness that makes teaching, like any other art, so complex an undertaking. Without automaticity and the ability to call on stock responses, energies are lost and inventiveness is hampered. (p. 176)

Teaching is less overwhelming to the experienced teacher in part because her repertoire of automatic practice is much more developed than that of the beginner: mental space is freed up to think of other things.

Reflection-in/on-action is not scripted but is action unique to a particular context. The interesting question then becomes: what triggers a teacher to move out of a script and respond uniquely to a context? What triggers thought beyond the script?

THE FRAMEWORKS FOR PRACTICE IN THE DIALOGIC OF TEACHING

To my surprise in working with teachers and attempting to understand their practice, I discovered (and discoveries always feel new to the owner, however apparent to others) that the teacher's sense of herself as teacher, her teaching identity, is not necessarily unitary, but continuously negotiated in context, and that it contains contradictory discourses or frameworks that "live and breathe" through her practice. These can be multiple (and no, she is not suffering from multiple-personality disorder), as the agenda competing for her actions, her response, is multiple, and she may not be able to acknowledge these contradictory practices. Her talk, for instance, may reflect one discourse or framework for action and her actions may include another. In other words, the teacher can be seen as a site of conflict in which contradictory discourses compete for space as lived practice. As Britzman (1991) argues, teaching is dialogic:

> Produced because of social interaction, subject to negotiation, consent, and circumstance, inscribed with power and desire, and always in the process of becoming, these dialogic relations determine the very texture of teaching and the possibilities it opens. (pp. 2–3)

Understanding the multiplicity of elements that enter and are negotiated by the teacher acting in the teaching world can permit us to reconceptualize this dialogic in teaching as a struggle for voice, for agency — the right to take action — amid, as Britzman says, "a cacophony of past and present voices, lived experiences, and available practices" (p. 8). If we think of the teacher as continuously negotiating her way through this multiplicity of factors competing for her attention, both helping to shape and being shaped by the complexity of the surrounding context, then we can understand teaching as much more complex than some straightforward notion of having a goal and implementing it, as the instrumentalists would have it.

The contradictions, for instance, in beliefs, values, and frameworks and the day-to-day enacting of practices that encapsulate these demonstrates how teachers are sites of conflict: the early childhood teacher becomes a set of contested selves — think of Jill telling a child not to crumple up tissue shapes one moment and saying it is all right in the next — and this is part of the burden of stress of teaching, the teacher's worry whether she is "doing the right thing." To act at all she must have some notion that her actions fit some imagined rightness, a singular truth, even as she negotiates among incompatible or conflicting ones.

"Teaching is fundamentally a dialogic relation, characterized by mutual dependency, social interaction and engagement" (Britzman, 1991, p. 237). To gain a sense of what is meant by a notion of a dialogic relation, I think of the metaphor of the self as a kaleidoscope, holding in view (whether explicitly or tacitly, as lived practice) the myriad fragments — voices of the past, bits of background experience, myths of expectation, interpretations of what is immediately required by the context, recognition of one's own need and so forth — that form the patterned network or web or labyrinth out of which choice of action (tacit or overt) must be derived. To understand teaching as a dialogic relation, then, is to see that much in teaching can be contradictory, that there is no necessary unitary stance, that even a clear image of practice is always contested, an ideal against which a multiplicity of teacher expectations, needs, and interpretations are played out, personally evaluated, and found wanting or rewarding. Contradictions offer several options to a teacher, and she must sift them, bring up one to which she can frame an allegiance for the moment, in order to act.

In this book, I have lifted out from the complexity of teaching relations one contradiction for our examination, and this is the contradiction between the two principal frameworks for action, teacher dominion and developmental appropriateness, encapsulated in the world of early childhood teaching. In doing so I do not mean to minimize the impact of other factors that contribute to shaping the practice of teachers. Systemic constraints in particular have an impact and salience seldom sufficiently recognized because they are so frequently taken for granted as normal, expected elements. The organization of time in schedules is a good example, as is the number of children imposed on the teacher by her administration. However, in this book I have reduced the role of systemic constraints to part of the backdrop, except in one story where they emerge irreparably and help to destroy teacher practice. For each teacher, there is a brief section acknowledging the constraints that she herself recognized in discussing her teaching. Otherwise, I prefer to keep the overwhelming impact of systemic constraints on early childhood practice for treatment elsewhere.

What I hope will become vivid as this book is read is the sense that while teachers may want to construct developmentally appropriate practice and may in fact believe that they do, many are constantly struggling with scripts for action in their setting that arise out of constraints in their work (scheduling, adult–child ratios and teacher shifts, physical elements such as the distance to the bathroom, and so forth) or out of the framework of teacher dominion. They may or may not be aware of this, and the particular scripts may or may not be of their own devising, but the patterns are present and have to be dealt with. What happens when the scripts in a setting display teacher-centered practice and the teacher wants to construct developmentally appropriate practice? What happens when practice is a mixture of both frameworks? What happens when someone with experience in teacher dominion enters a setting where developmental appropriateness is valued? These are the things we will see.

Each chapter that follows tells a story—some are positive and exciting, some are difficult and sad—and I have used the data to serve the overall theme of the chapter. But the data always show much more than is discussed. We all can see this: it is this which permits readers to enter the story and participate in their own interpretations.

Extracting this book from a doctoral dissertation was like unraveling a finished coat and knitting it into a sweater. In the thesis, I discussed four arguments showing what makes the construction of developmentally appropriate practice difficult for early childhood educators. The four arguments can be summarized as follows:

1. Teachers may have allegiances to several frameworks simultaneously, each prescribing different responses to children and how they learn, and shift back and forth in action from one framework to another.
2. Teachers inherited and planned scripts for action using the framework of teacher dominion without conscious intent, and they perpetuated these as expected practice.
3. Teachers were sometimes unfamiliar not only with the concepts of developmentally appropriate practice (which they nevertheless tended to value) but with the performance skills or scripts for action to put it into practice.
4. External constraints imposing on teachers could, through intensification of work, obstruct opportunities to construct developmentally appropriate practice.

These elements do not exist separately in a teacher's work. Thus here I want to reassemble those elements and show how they interweave, how dynamic practice is, so that if one element is changed, the outcome would be different. Events happen not from simple cause and effect but from the impact of a multiplicity of threads interweaving and bearing on each other, as individuals act and react to the flow of experience that surrounds them.

While each case is specific and unique to its particular place and time, in that even if I returned to these same participants their stories would now be different, they do, when seen together, permit the similar threads to show through. Each teacher must deal with the very real external constraints imposing on her practice. Each teacher must manage group processes, make materials accessible, shepherd children through some sort of routine. Each teacher will have scripted patterns of action, possibly unrecognized as such by her, and will engage in them as if they are the foundation of the teaching world. Each teacher will reflect at certain moments when events trigger a disposition to problem solve rather than act routinely. But what specifics of context trigger it in this teacher, not in the other? What scripts does she use and how does she change them? How does she manage group processes? Above all, how can we assist teachers in gaining a sense of mastery about their teaching?

I believe this can be done in part through making explicit the dynamics of quotidian work life as they existed for specific teachers. Such stories of practice help to remove the isolation in which teachers of young children work and reveal the burdens and special problems of early childhood work, as well as its rewards. What we can see is the common elements of practice from teacher to teacher and the myriad, richly textured ways these interweave to construct the social world of early childhood classrooms. Goffin (1989) attributes to Schulman the observation that teaching "lacks a history of practice—that no collective memory of teachers' best practices exists (similar to architectural plans and buildings, legal case studies, or medical records)" (p. 199) and suggests we should collect and interpret the practical knowledge of teachers. This is what I have tried to do in what follows, to bring into the open the complexities of practice as it exists, so that we can see the struggles of teachers to build the best practice they can for children and to master their own work.

2 One Teacher, Two Frameworks for Action

Jill valued and constructed both teacher dominion and developmentally appropriate practice in her work in a day care setting: this chapter shows one way that this split allegiance to two different frameworks can occur in a classroom, the tensions that result for the teacher, and her direction toward resolving them. It was not the case that Jill consciously set out to construct such a practice, of course, but that this was what we discovered during the period of my research with her. She described herself as "following the footsteps" [J2.5], that is, taking up the pattern of activities that was in place in the setting when she joined it: "well that was the way it was when I came, and I guess I think that's the way it should be done, so that's the way I do it" [J1.17]. In other words, she accepted and adopted the scripted patterns of action already in place in the setting and assumed these as the bedrock of her practice.

What was the way it was? As you will hear, time was organized like traditional school, with fixed time periods for separate activities, thus supporting teacher-centered practice. On the other hand, Jill believed children should always be active and involved, and that she should offer choices and ensure their active engagement with materials and people. She thought activities should belong to children, that she should play with them. Let's go into her room and first gain a sense of the ambience she creates, and then recognize the several constraints which impose on her efforts. Then we can explore the tensions in her work and see how, in part, they arise out of the scripts for teacher-centered practice that she stepped into, and how she is resolving these tensions.

Jill cares for 14 children, 2 to 4 years of age, and has worked in the same room and with the same co-worker, Marion, since she began day care teaching 9 years ago. Prior to her day care work, she took a 10-month training program in early childhood education following high school. With her love of visual display (Jill always wore such interesting earrings), she worked first selling ladies clothes at a department store; she began working in day care almost by chance, when asked to substitute in the center where she had completed her practicum. She has been there ever since. Jill is quiet and reserved, and moves about her setting with qualities of grace and refinement.

Her room is light, with windows on two sides and a movable step so children can look out. One free play time, Geoffrey spent most of it excitedly watching blackbirds flapping at a milk carton birdfeeder which they had made and hung outside the window. The room is very clean and organized, "a place for everything," says Jill. One end has a cozy area with books, record player, Lego and puzzles, and a single fish in a tank. The other has a table area, with sandbox nearby and a dramatic play area in the middle. There are small changes to the room each time I come, a minitrampoline or slide added, a different set of 14 collage papers on the bulletin board, once a mural of African animals when they pretended to go to Africa as a theme. Children's songs waft frequently from the record player, and there is singing and dancing. Here we see Jill for a moment as she encourages children to put on smocks before craft: some children whine and complain they cannot do it.

"You try, I'll help you in a minute. Find the holes for your arms." One child gets it over her head successfully. "Yeah, Eliza, when you try you can do it! You guys are catching on so fast. It makes it much easier if everybody tries" [JF2.2].

OVERVIEW OF JILL'S PROGRAM

Jill's program was characterized by two major contexts, each with a different set of expectations about what she and the children would be doing. One context was what she termed "free play," and the other was teacher-centered group activity. I will describe both free play and group times, trying to give the feel of the alternating rhythms of activity in her class.

The matrix in which all activity in the setting was held was a school-like design for using time. Time was divided into tight compartments with specific activities slotted into them like shoes in a shoebox.

> I come in at 9:30 and we tidy up and have snack. And from 9:30 to 10:00 we do snack and bathroom to finish right at 10:00 so it's not too early. 'Cause today we were finished at 10 to 10, so then it kind of makes the morning longer? So then at 10 we tidy up, and I take half the children and do craft, and Marion has the other [half] and she does circle for 20 minutes and then we rotate the groups. [J1.1]

Her description of the day continues in this fashion, with time and activity parceled out into boxes of 20 to 30 minutes until she leaves at 5:30 in the afternoon. Activities were the "figure" to be distinguished from the "ground" of the time slots they filled. Sometimes the content of the time box was to meet basic needs — snack, lunch, nap, bathroom — and otherwise it was free play (three segments during Jill's work) alternating with teacher-centered activity conducted for the group.

There are several possible ways to build activities into a day, for instance, by whim, by plan, or by the clock. Ball, Hull, Skelton, and Tudor (1984) note that "a modern industrial conception of time is strongly present in schools, where timetabling symbolizes the finite, ordered and scarce nature of 'school time'" (p. 41). The teacher in schools is the master timekeeper for the class, controlling the content and pace, and in turn responding to the schoolwide time frame authored by the administration. Ball and associates argue that the organization of time becomes taken for granted as part of the meaning of school and that teachers then cannot imagine anything different: it would not be recognizable as part of their definition of school. Jackson's (1968/1990) insights into the hidden curriculum of schools demonstrated how children learn to wait passively and to repress self-initiated learning in order to give over agency to the teacher. For Ball and associates the impact of this experience is such that "time as a regulator of activities in school may provide a basic socialization into subordination to time regulation in other institutional contexts" (p. 57). I argue that Jill's tacit acceptance of the time structure is an example of this.

Since this familiar pattern for organizing time was already in place in the setting when Jill began her work, she acquired a set of taken-for-granted scripts for her role vis-à-vis time: she is the timekeeper, the keeper of the routine through which children are shepherded. How do we know this is part of the substrata of assumptions about her work? We can see it in part through the dynamic of the way time intersects with other elements, as in the following example.

Jill's program planning was based on themes whose content was slotted into presentations in teacher-directed groups. One of Jill's themes was a week devoted to pretending to visit Africa. A parent brought in a book of African games that Jill told me could not be used because the week was almost over. "She didn't bring that until Thursday, I think, so we really couldn't use that" [J5.9]. With this conception of how time and content intersect, carrying African games (or the entire safari) over into the next week was inconceivable; the time segment was gone and another succeeded it, different and at odds with it. Content is inserted in time, which is conceived as a kind of train that one catches or misses, and this conception was part of the "ground" that informed how Jill constructed her work.

I have said her program planning centered on themes. She planned what she wanted the children to learn, using group times to convey content — shapes, colors, the alphabet, numbers, seasons, and so forth. Children should "recognize the colors" in a color song, pick up new words and the specific idea of a story, "grab the concept of trees or plants or something" [J1.19]. Beyond the explicit content, she wanted them to learn to sit quietly, not to bother those around them, to speak as requested and be silent as requested: the purpose of show and tell, for instance, was described as "for language skills" and "being able to speak in front, getting up in front of their friends" [J5.2]. Here we see indirect instruction in the framework in which many traditional school activities are held, 2- and 3-year-olds undergoing tacit preparation to accept the structure of school time and the framework of school activity, where question and answer is often considered a primary technique of instruction.

At the same time she finds the traditional curriculum content she has been using for themes — shapes, colors, alphabet, and numbers — (which is remarkably similar to the content of traditional kindergarten and primary classrooms) increasingly boring: "like doing 'Fall,' I get so bored doing 'Fall,' every fall I don't want to do it anymore" [J1.12]. (She keeps on because her colleague likes it.) Many themes she has done over and over, trying to find some different activities that make it bearable for her. Yet even though she was bored with themes, Jill believed she should be doing them for the children's sake because she values the content and young children's exposure to it. She told me that in one other room in her center there were "artsy" teachers who did "really weird themes" but she thought they should be doing "Numbers" and "Fall." I asked her why she thought they should be doing those themes.

> I guess down in the other group because they're going to be starting school next year. With us, just I guess make them aware of numbers. I guess stuff that they always use when they're in school? . . . Just I guess so they'll be aware of them now. . . . I want them to know their colors, their numbers. [J6.5–6]

Jill sees a part of her role as familiarizing children with material they will encounter in school. Implicitly, she wants to prepare them for this content, whether or not the school would see this as necessary. These themes, provided in a routine that simulates conventional school processes and approximates school content, have the purpose of preparation. Teacher-centered group activities, using scripts for teacher dominion, are thus a rehearsal for school, several years before the actual experience.

But because of her boredom with content, Jill read new books, looking for new ideas for craft or circle or themes (finding one, for instance, on problem solving), and this tendency to seek out new material brought her into contact with ideas that contrasted with her teacher-directed program and that she also valued.

Jill also believed that children should be fully active, involved in what they were doing, with ample opportunity to engage in a lively way with material. But these beliefs are theoretically mutually exclusive: children cannot be waiting and active simultaneously. To wait is to withhold activity. To be active is to impose one's own agenda on material. Developmentalists argue that a 2-year-old cannot inhibit activity; without physical engagement nothing much can happen. Teacher-centered proponents teach waiting and taking turns to facilitate group functioning, to prevent chaos, and to permit a single thread of activity to connect the group. Jill believes in both, and this second set of beliefs and practices emerges in "free play."

For Jill, free play described children's freedom to choose the activity they wished from those available. Her actions at this time had multiple functions: she participated in play, if she was able (particularly in music), or "eating lunch" in housekeeping, if asked; she assisted children in and out of dress-up clothes (most children were under age 3), or with fastening Lego or stacking blocks, not imposing ideas but assisting children's efforts; she might sit and listen, because "it's interesting," as she did with Sandy, who went up the loft stairs saying she was off to the baseball game. Here we see her for a few minutes during free play.

After group time, Jill puts Raffi on the record player and joins the children to march and sing. Trevor bangs the drum with a confident beat, Lisa bangs sticks randomly, and Jill marches with them, clanging sticks as she goes. Then she tells them they can do something in the rest of the room now, if they wish, or they can stay and dance. Suddenly, she crosses the room and sets out three paint pots and brushes at places around a table. Three girls follow her and paint; two boys stay to drum and dance.

Sandy kneels at the flannelboard easel and Jill comes, reaches into its inside without a word, and pulls out a huge child-sized Charlie Brown figure with cut-out felt clothes; the child presses pieces of felt around the figure. Several children draw, after painting, replacing the marker tops carefully. Jill joins a child who asks "Can I have the rain song?" They sing with the song, and as the others finish drawing, they come, drawn by the sound. Three girls and Jill sing the 'paw paw patch' song, each with a turn to hide and be found. They insist Jill take a turn hiding, too, and she crawls under the loft. All three run to find her, falling into her arms for a big hug.

Jill gets up, comes out from under the loft, saying: "Is Mallory still painting over there?" They all troop over to the table. "Oh what a lovely picture." [J4.4–5]

Overriding her involvement with individual children is the need to monitor the whole group, ensure its smooth functioning. This requires watching everybody, "running back and forth" as Jill describes it, and then taking action where it is judged necessary. When would she intervene? An argument among children, a child wandering and in need of encouragement to play or find something to do — these would draw her. As well, she actively sees that children are spaced comfortably within her room, adding materials that invite them into activity and placing them evenly, so that children are not bunched or crowded together in one locale.

All the materials and areas were always open to children during free play, and this was her preference, "so they can pick what they want" [J5.18]. Child choice thus was important to her. She actively invited children into play with suggestions such as "Do you want to play Mr. Potato Head?" or by putting paint, playdough, matching games out on tables after circle, or by responding inmmediately to requests such as "Can I have the rain song?"

She also continuously demonstrated the techniques for doing things — how to hold a straw to dab paint, how to move a chair, how to clean up spilled flour, how to say "excuse me" on the stairs. Constantly, through paying attention to aspects of children's actions, she modeled how she wanted things done and people treated in her room — with respect, good manners, gentleness.

CONSTRAINTS IN JILL'S PRACTICE

During the 9-month period of my contact with Jill, the constraints that make teacher work more difficult were neither bothersome nor compelling for her. Her room offered everything she wanted, except for running water, but she and her colleague had worked out a system for access to this. According to her description, she had no difficult children at this time and was not overburdened with student teachers. Her long years of work with the same colleague in the same environment, and a manageable number of children, meant that her situation was one of stability and comfort. There were only two arenas of constraint that offered her some difficulty.

Each of these constraints resulted in an uncomfortable intensification of work. The teacher-centered group segments, hung on the frame of school-like organization of time, resulted in intensification due to time pressure, the necessity of accomplishing the routine. The more developmentally appropriate segments, built upon the foundation of child choice and pace, resulted, when combined with the reality of staff–child ratios, in an intensification of work from the necessity of monitoring all the children while alone. We will look first at the time problem, then the monitoring one.

The result of the shoebox time slots for activities was a rush to be ready for the next one. In cleaning up between craft groups, for instance, Jill would be "trying to get everything put away and the table cleaned up before everybody comes out [from her colleague's 'circle'] and Marion goes on break" [J1.18]; this included hanging up paper products, monitoring children who were finished and playing, and helping those who were still occupied at the craft table. Giroux and Penna (1981) note that:

> The concept of time in schools restricts the development of healthy social and intellectual relationships among students and teachers. Reminiscent of life in factories with its production schedules and hierarchical work relationships, the daily routine of most classrooms acts as a brake upon participation and democratic processes. (p. 225)

For Jill, her rush to be ready for the next group foreclosed on child participation in cleaning up in a relaxed way and on any sense of inhabiting the activity. The activity's pace was controlled by the clock, and Jill worked frantically during the transition to be ready for the next group.

The second major constraint upon her practice was the requirement that she monitor children during free play as the sole person responsible for them. Jill was alone with 14 children for 30 minutes of morning free play, and, with somewhat reduced numbers of children, 30 minutes of afternoon free play. This was approximately two-thirds of her free-play time with the children, a situation resulting from the need to accommodate teachers' breaks [J3.12–13]. The practice of building a teacher break into the time schedule during free play had the impact on practice of intensifying her responsibility to monitor everyone and reducing her involvement with children.

When asked what her overall purpose was with the children, Jill said simply that she was there to play with the children and she would much prefer to be able to play with them more, but the need to monitor interferes and she is not able to interact much in the children's play.

> Well I feel I would rather be playing with them, interacting with them more, but I don't see any way to do that. Without, well, I'm trying to watch them all at the same time. [J3.13]

I'm basically, when I'm alone, I'm not really involved in their free play. I'm just watching them to make sure everything's okay. [J3.12]

My major argument here is to show how Jill in her thinking and action was attached almost equally to both teacher dominion and developmental appropriateness, how she used both and shifted between them, but I do not wish to oversimplify her work. For in free play, in which she believed she should be interacting more actively with the children — a practice promoted by developmental appropriateness — these possibilities were truncated, fragmented by her responsibility for monitoring 14 young children alone.

THE TENSION BETWEEN TWO
FRAMEWORKS FOR TEACHER ACTION

A tension in the work of a day care teacher is a system of relationships that pulls her simultaneously in different directions, toward conflicting ways of thinking and acting. Such tensions produce implicit dilemmas, places where she must choose one course of action over other possibilities. To concretize the notion of such tensions, think of a spider constructing not one but two webs. One is constructed perpendicular to the other so that each occupies space in a different direction, each has its own plane, and the two do not interfere with each other except where individual threads abut across a single diagonal in each web. Metaphors as images of mental frameworks have sudden-death limits, but I use the image to introduce the notion of a pivot point. The pivot point is a place where the two webs abut, and the hypothetical spider has to decide whether to continue in the space and time provided by one structure or whether to cross over into the other. It cannot do both, and it must make a move, so what is required is a split-second decision to go in one direction or the other.

As I observed several participants — Sonia, Jill, Nora — and as I went over the interview transcripts and thought about the videotapes we had shared, I recognized that there were times when I could see them visibly struggling between two different directions at once, brought about not by the conflicting demands of the multiple agenda — for there were numerous occasions when there were two or more things to be done — but by their own sense of what to do in the context. These moments, in particular, reflected a seesawing back and forth between two conflicting ideas or images about practice. I call these pivot points.

A pivot point is a moment in time/space in which the teacher is torn between two ways of acting, each reflecting a different mental image or framework for action. (I see a dilemma for teachers as any broad, sweeping tension that continues to accompany their work: the pivot point, in contrast, is a particularized moment in practice that will never happen again in exactly the same fashion.) In watching and talking to Jill, for instance, it was possible to see that sometimes she decided to move in the direction that showed allegiance to one framework, and sometimes in the other. This idea of pivot points emerged through the interaction of several data collection strategies — interviews, reviewing together videotaped segments of her program, reading and discussing the feedback paper constructed from observations and interviews. It was the process of reviewing her own actions, either on videotape or as displayed in my written feedback, and then reacting, which revealed those points that were pivots for a particular teacher. These were places where she could see herself moving in one direction, but wishing she'd done something else, or while in the midst of one approach, suddenly switching to another. These two different ways of doing things, which Jill generally kept in separate time compartments, met head-on in several specific activities, as we will see. These contexts or time slots were craft, show and tell, and cooking, in which the conflict between teacher dominion and a more developmental approach saw Jill shifting back and forth in her decisions about what to do from moment to moment.

Crumpled Tissue Shapes

The dilemma for Jill during craft time was whether child-initiated process or teacher direction should or would predominate. One morning, Jill presented the children with collage materials to glue to a background, multicolored tissue pieces precut into small geometric shapes. Her expectations for what they should do with these suggested both an acceptance of child process and a concern that children learn her theme content.

> I think they should be noticing the shapes and glueing them on. Not necessarily making anything constructive — which they did do — I just thought maybe a collage of shapes. Looking at them, and maybe discussing them, and sticking them on. [J2.6]

A direction of developmental appropriateness was present here in the lack of concern for a specified product and an apparent tolerance of child process. She also wanted evidence that she was getting across her theme content: she wanted shape discrimination and talk which reflected this.

From a jar of tissue shapes, Jill pulls out handfuls and distributes
them, sorting through the ones in her hand to provide each child
some variety of shapes, finding a triangle for this one, a circle for
that. Wanda blows her shapes around the table, flipping them over
the paper. The children begin to glue at once. Wanda crumples tissue
pieces up in her fists, making little wadded bits. Jill tells her, "You're
scrunching them up. I want you to leave them open so you can see
the shape." She bends over Wanda, helping her smooth out the bits.
[JF2.3]

When the child-initiated process of crumpling tissue infringed on the in-
tegrity of the tissue shape, Jill intervened to correct Wanda in order to
preserve her focus on shape. We see, in a split second of practice, how the
concern for learning, the focus she has selected, takes on more priority for
her than the child's process, and she used teacher direction to alter it. In
this moment, she was following the web, the mental framework, suggested
by teacher dominion. However, this same incident recurred with a different child later in the craft time, and she told this child it was "alright to
have them crumpled on the paper, sometimes they look nice that way"
[J2.3]. In that moment of decision, she stepped into the other web, permitting the child-initiated process of actions on the material.

This tension occurred numerous times for Jill in craft, and she made
the decision to act sometimes in one direction, sometimes in the other,
favoring first teacher-centered practice, then developmentally appropriate
practice, or vice versa. This tension was evident, too, when she described
an unsuccessful activity:

Or maybe sometimes you're doing craft and you have something in
your mind, and they have something totally different in their mind,
and it's like — but it's right, I mean, it's fine. They can do what
they're doing. But you kind of wish they'd do it another way, you
know. [J1.20]

She succinctly states the dilemma of whether her idea (the planned one)
or theirs (the result of child-initiated process) should prevail. She tolerates
their ideas with some ambivalence, wishing nevertheless for a better
match between her idea and their product. The "Frosty the Snowman"
collages on the bulletin board in December illustrate her dilemma. She
had precut three white circles of varying size and red rectangular hat and
scarf pieces and provided black background paper: the children (all 2-
and 3-year-olds) glued all the pieces randomly on the papers. Adults could
catch her intention — snowmen — merely from the cutout shapes. Whether

the children thought to make snowmen is unclear. Perhaps they did, and at their age saw no need for a conventional ordering of parts to convey the image: intention is enough. Or perhaps they merely glued the pieces without intention.

Throughout our observations and interviews, Jill's decisions around this pivot point would be first in one direction, then the other. The tension seemed balanced, her movement like a seesaw — first this side, then the other, with each appearing equally preferred in her talk and actions. However, when we met again 3 months later and she read the feedback paper, she wrote beside a description of the incident where she corrected Wanda for crumpling tissue shapes: "I shouldn't have done this, I should have let them crumple the tissue paper if they chose to" [Jper14]. She added verbally, "because that's the way she wanted to do it." She told me then that she had changed, that she was letting them "stretch more, get away with more, do more, I guess, on their own" in craft [J6.4]. She reported that this came about in part from watching the videotape. With these comments, she showed herself to be leaning in the direction of favoring more child-centered practice, giving up control where she sees she does not need to keep it.

Monkeybread

Baking time was an another example of a context in which Jill felt the dilemma of the pull between child-centered process and teacher-centered instruction. One morning I videotaped Jill conducting a baking time with a small group of five children. All the ingredients were neatly assembled on a tray adjacent to the table. Each child was presented with a saucer, a spoon or fork, and a segment of banana to mash up. This was of some challenge, and the children worked intently poking and prodding the slippery bananas and eventually subduing them on the saucer, flattened. Then, each child was offered a turn to pour and stir an ingredient for the bread into the bowl. This resulted in four children watching and waiting as one acted. Walter kept up a continuous barrage of "My turn, when's it my turn!" [J3.2] each time the bowl moved from one child to the next.

When Jill and I watched this on video, she broke in with:

I don't really enjoy baking that often, . . . because they all have to sit there and wait their turn and it's a long time to go around. [J3.2]

Oh I get frustrated, and I think they do, waiting for their turn. And to see. They can't really see, and they want to see, they want to be doing things constantly. [J3.4]

Here Jill is caught between her belief, consonant with developmental appropriateness, that children need to be continuously active in interacting with materials and people, and a favoring of teacher dominion that required waiting and following teacher instructions. She attempted to provide ongoing activity by ensuring each child had material to work with, a banana to mash. Then in the teacher-directed segment of preparing the batter for baking, the part that required a sequence, she was frustrated because the children had to wait their turn to be active. Learning to wait to be active was not something Jill wanted children to endure: "I think they have to be doing something" [J3.8]. Yet in group activities such as circle, show and tell, and baking, conducted primarily in a teacher-centered fashion, waiting was inevitable. The pivot point here is activity versus passivity. She did not want them to have to wait, passive; and in this instance, her frustration was exacerbated by the child who constantly repeated that he needed a turn.

As we watched the video, she verbalized a series of reflections on what else she might do to counteract this problem.

> Maybe I could have started with Walter first. I wonder if that would have made a difference. It probably wouldn't have, because he still would have to wait. But if he'd been next to me, it might have made a difference. But he'd still have to wait. [J3.6]

> Well I think next time I might do it, I might try standing up.
> *How do you think that will change it?*
> Well I think they might be able to see better. Possibly. And I might try something where they can all have their own thing[s]. . . . I usually do one thing and they all do it. [J3.8–9]

As Jill thinks of providing individual materials for each child, as she does in craft, she appears to lean in the direction of preferring developmentally appropriate practice. Her preferred value that children should be active at all times is in tension with her preferred structure for conducting group activities, which consistently used teacher-centered practice.

However, in watching the video, Jill found it *looked* quite different than it had felt to her when she was engaged in it.

> I think they enjoyed it. . . . It was really different seeing it. And they were stirring, and really getting into it, and watching everything that was going on. When I did it, waiting for each one to have a turn, to me it seemed like it was *long*. But watching it, it didn't seem as long. [J3.8]

The tension between her belief in teacher instruction to wait, take turns, as necessary for the activity, and her belief that children require continuous activity with materials conflicted in this activity (as perhaps it might not in group activities where there are no materials), creating a pivot point around her decision to bake or not: she would offer a weekly baking occasion for some time and then let it "slide down" [J6.4]. However, at our final interview, she told me she had continued to bake every week, and I infer that it was in part the effect of seeing this segment on video, seeing the children interested and involved even as they merely watched, that increased her confidence in the activity.

Although Jill used teacher-centered practice in group time as the foundation of her program, she equally valued children's control over their own actions, child choice of process. This implicit belief emerged in her tendency to give children small moments of choice in group times, such as letting them change the actions of a song or the time Elizabeth didn't want to demonstrate her turquoise plastic slinky the way Jill suggested. Jill invited her to show them how it worked by sliding it back and forth from palm to palm of her hands. Elizabeth said oh no, her hands were too small, she would show them on the loft stairs [J5.14]. This implicit belief in sharing control with children had an interesting impact on the tightly held boundaries between teacher-centered segments and free play. Stories, library books, and music activities were all conducted initially in teacher-directed fashion. But after Jill's presentation, library books would be set on a table during free play, and after a song circle, children would be invited to stay and sing and dance on their own during free play. This seesaw balancing of control, now the teacher's turn, now the child's across time contexts, occurred most vividly for theme content and music.

Show and Tell

In the third context in which the tension was most evident, show and tell, Jill had been shifting toward a more developmental approach, conscious of child process and intention, and this was clearly in conflict with the way she had been conducting this as school-like instruction.

> When we first did show and tell, it was whoever was showing could show, and the rest had to sit quietly and watch. I would say "It's Wanda's turn, wait till she's finished." But then, they want to say stuff. [J5.10]

But she had changed it by the time I was working with her, so that the occasion looked something like this:

Jill conducts show and tell with six children whom she bodily places in a loose semicircle around the shopping bag of items. A Mickey Mouse stuffed animal is first. "Come on up here, Chloe, and show everybody what you brought." "Mickey Mouse." "What's hanging on the string?" "It's a bear," says Daniel. After each item is displayed by the child, talked up by the teacher, it is parked at the circle's edge, near John. At one point, his fingers flex over a large-beaded fake pearl necklace. He rubs his palm over the beads, curling them up in his fingers. Jill takes up the necklace and passes it around the group again, inviting them to feel it, try it on. [JF5.7, JV4]

In this circle, she switched away from her focus on language skills as she talked with children about the toys, and she invited more interaction with the necklace when a child showed interest. As we watched this on video, she commented: "How hard it must be to sit there. Like I think, imagine if you're sitting there, and there's a bunch of fudge [next you] and you're not allowed to touch it" [J5.10]? Here she broke from the tradition of expecting children to sit and listen while another talks and invited them to handle material, feel its texture, try it around their necks; and she did this as a result of seeing John's desire to touch the necklace. In other words, she slipped over to the developmental side, seeing the children's need for active engagement with concrete materials.

As well, she kept the group small, let them play with the items afterward, let them discuss the objects among each other: "I've been changing by letting them play with them or passing stuff around, letting the others speak" [J5.10]. She was relaxing the teacher-taught framework to permit more child participation and control, instituting a mini–free play with the collected toys among the small group. She noted that for the children the most salient aspect of the occasion is the novel toys, "and they just want to play with them" [J5.3]. Talking in a more conversational way, playing more, and more child participation all led to a show and tell that was less formal in structure, more open to child-initiated activity. For Jill this remains a dilemma. "It's hard to figure out which way to do it, but it's for *them*. Of course, I don't know which way Marion does it either" [J5.10]. There is worry here, tension between her belief in the children's right to the activity as their own and belief in the structure of teacher-taught episodes, content-driven and with objectives such as language development and ease of speaking before a group. There is also the revelation that she had not discussed this with her colleague, although they communicated constantly about the children. It was in the context of show and tell that these tensions between two conflicting sets of beliefs about what children should be doing were most pronounced.

RECOGNITION OF ALLEGIANCE TO TWO FRAMEWORKS

I wrote about this allegiance to two frameworks, two images of practice, in the feedback paper for Jill, and I surfaced this with some trepidation, for we had not discussed this: it emerged in analysis. Why, when it is a dilemma that seems so obvious once it is raised, had we not previously seen it? It seemed to me that these two frameworks each offered specific scripts for action implied by their values and understanding of children and that the ways of enacting these in practice become automatic, a substrata of competing forms of tacit knowledge that the teacher believes reflect how the world works. Polanyi (1958) states this well:

> When we accept a certain set of pre-suppositions and use them as our interpretive framework we may be said to dwell in them as we do in our own body. Their uncritical acceptance for the time being consists in a process of assimilation by which we identify ourselves with them. . . . As they are themselves our ultimate framework, they are essentially inarticulable. (p. 60)

In Jill's setting, each framework occurred in its own separate time frame, teacher dominion and developmental appropriateness in an alternating rhythm. The notion that developmentally appropriate practice could extend across the entire day, or suggest a different handling of time, was beyond, as Greene (1988) would say, Jill's horizon of understanding, her vision of the possible.

What happens, then, when someone like a researcher brings the presence of not one but two competing frameworks as prescriptive of teacher action out into the open? Jill reacted to the argument that she operates with two frameworks with recognition. After reading the feedback paper, when I asked how this argument struck her, she said with shining eyes, "That's me!"

The tension between two frameworks for action in her work processes, which Jill acknowledged with recognition, did not affect the climate of psychological safety and comfort in her room: it was a happy, relaxed place to visit. Jill's corrections, for instance, were so polite and respectful of children, and while I was visiting, there were no conflicts between a teacher and a child. To recall the quality of her relationship with the children, think of them insisting she have a turn in the "paw paw patch" song and enfolding her in a hug when they found her under the loft.

Jill said she was bored with the theme content taught in teacher-directed ways. As an observer and former teacher, my sense was the same:

the content, while pleasant, felt a little thin, shallow, old hat. However, as she permitted child-initiated activity, suddenly (like dogs perking up their ears) everyone was alert and engaged. At our final interview, it was clear that as she let children "get away with more" in craft, and opened up show and tell toward more ownership of activity by the children, that those moment-by-moment decisions were shifting in the direction of practice that was increasingly developmentally appropriate. As an outsider with whom Jill shared her teaching, I wondered when this shift would reach a threshold that might bring the time structure of school into question, and what her story would be now, since she has become a mother twice over since our work together.

3 | Teacher Dominion and Multiple Constraints

Sonia's work was built upon teacher dominion almost in entirety — to the point that she considered free play a spare period in which to accomplish teacher tasks — and she was somewhat unfamiliar with developmentally appropriate practice. Multiple and pressing constraints imposed on whatever practice she might construct. The shock for both of us occurred when, 3 months after our 5 months of visits and interviews, I returned with a feedback paper describing her practical knowledge and invited her reaction to it. She was startled by my portrayal of her, for she thought she was much more child-centered than her practice indicated. What I want to show here is how the combination of teacher-centered practice and the weight of constraints together had unexpected consequences for Sonia, for the children in her care, and for her sense of herself as teacher.

We began our research together in early October, when she was 1 month into a new job in day care, but it is important to note that, ultimately, she wanted to teach elementary school. She had come to this job in day care after 2 years of work in a preschool program and was a graduate of a 4-year university program that combined child study with a bachelor of education degree. Sonia nevertheless did not find her preparation adequate: "I don't think my training really helped me in going in and working in a day care. . . . It was more a lot about theories. . . . I don't think I draw on my training very much when I'm working" [S7.9]. In contrast, she thought her approach as a day care teacher had been "molded" by the teacher with whom she had just finished working for 2 years.

What was this new job in day care? In the mornings Sonia conducted a "nursery school" for 3-year-olds. Most children attended only several mornings a week, so the roster of children changed daily. There might be 7 to 12 on any given day, with 10 about average. These children went home at noon, when 34 children ages 5 to 10 arrived from a variety of nearby public and private schools for lunch. (The school board in this metropolitan area does not keep children through the lunch hour.) They returned to school shortly after one o'clock.

Then 7 "primaries" (5-year-olds who did not return to school in the afternoon) had a program with one teacher while the other was on lunch break. As the year progressed, these children went back to school 2 days a week, remaining in the day care center the other 3. In January, other children from another location, 4-year-olds who did not nap, were added at this time to bring the group size to 10. Different children arrived to join the primaries each day, so Sonia did not know exactly who would appear. At three o'clock, these added-in children left, and the 34 school-agers returned, and an afterschool program was conducted until 5:30.

Sonia and her partner, Iris, thus had, in their view, three programs to construct and manage for three different age groups from age 2½ to 10 and a changing cast of players from day to day. To the outsider, it felt a little like going to a fair, people coming and going, the setting sometimes very noisy and crowded, sometimes sparsely populated. Adding to the fairlike atmosphere were spectacularly decorated bulletin board displays, every spare inch of wall space covered. In February, for instance, there were hearts everywhere, doilies on a valentine tree, pink hearts strewn with exuberance over the theme board, lunchbags stapled below in a row for each child's cards, huge cutout hearts emblazoned with "Love is . . . " along one wall. The furniture and materials stayed the same, but the walls changed weekly. The location was physically isolated from the rest of the center with the result that Sonia and Iris worked independently in an abundantly equipped and well-designed space.

OVERVIEW OF SONIA'S PROGRAM

What was Sonia's approach to this inflow and outflow of different groups of children all day? She held in place a complex routine of teacher-centered scripts for action, highly planned and outlined in a program book that was submitted to the administration once a week. She was, throughout our interviews, terribly concerned that this plan book be complete and well received — "our program has to be in our book" [S6.18] — and fretted over it frequently [S1.1, S1.9, S2.21, S2.5, S6.3–4]. While there was no positive feedback to her from the weekly submission, as long as the plan book came back initialed she knew there were no problems.

Her elaborate program planning centered on weekly themes, and she tried to prepare, for each group with which she worked, a daily teacher-directed circle, a craft, a song circle, and a movement activity, each in its own time frame. The pattern of organizing time was the school-like design, with an activity for each time slot. The format of these teacher-centered group activities was similar to conventional notions of teacher instruction in schools, that is, the session was obligatory for the children and in circles they listened and did as they were told, as we see here.

Sonia's theme for one week was shapes, and she had prepared paper puppets with faces and holes (so two fingers looked like legs) in the shape of a circle, rectangle, square, and triangle. She placed a puppet on her hand, named it, and asked the children to find things like it in the room.

"Can you think of something that is made out of a square?"
"A table?"
"A table could be made out of a square, what else?"
"Plates!"
"Music?" says one. [They had an old boxy record player in the room.]
"Is music a square? No. Can you think of anything else that's a square? Look around," says Sonia. The children and Sonia name items, the Exit sign, someone's lunchbox. One child shakes her hair vigorously back and forth, another raises and lowers her knees.
"How about this triangle?" Sonia holds up her paper puppet.
"A house!"
"Yes, the roof. When we were doing craft today we thought of something shaped like a triangle. Can you remember?" [No, they cannot.] "A musical instrument," says Sonia.
"Oh, yeah!" says one.
"What is it?"
"I don't know."
"A triangle, it's called a triangle, too." [SF3.2–3; SV1]

Circles were content-driven: "I first wanted to introduce them to the shapes, [and] to think about what things are made of certain shapes" [S3.10]. The surprise in this circle was that the children already knew the shapes: "I thought it was going to be a lot of trying to get to know these shapes; I hadn't expected them to know them very well" [S3.9, 11]. As Sonia said, circle was "basically talk time" [S1.14]. What, then, were children to do with the content presented to them? Sonia wanted them to learn it and also to grasp the underlying structure of group activities as a school-like process. "They learn about structure. They learn there's times when they have to sit and not be silly and talk and play and have fun. There's times to sit and think. I think they learn to listen" [S6.12]. Preparation for school, both in terms of the content of these activities and of understanding how they may be conducted was thus an implicit factor in using these activities with both 3- and 5-year-olds. Again, teacher-centered activity was a rehearsal for school.

In my research I found that when teacher-centered activity and school-time pervade day care practice, then "free play" tends to be approached as a fixed time for removing teacher direction and participation from children's activity. With teacher direction lifted off, the teacher stands back outside the play domain, intervening only for control reasons, such as conflict among children or management of space and materials. This absence of teacher participation in play was not seen as incompatible with a high valuing of the importance of play for children. Sonia, too, believed that play is very important for young children, among other reasons because children "learn to share, they socialize . . . they discover things" [S2.13–14], but that children can play on their own unless a problem requires adult intervention; apart from handling problems, she thought teacher involvement in play is unnecessary.

How did Sonia describe what she was occupied with during free play? She was busy signing children in, attending to forms, greeting and talking to children, and either "basically circling around" [S1.8] in general monitoring or doing a "free craft" with those who chose it. It was during free play that she found moments to make signs, "run out and tape the bills to their cubbies or clean a shelf" [S2.8]. The perceived need to attend to maintenance and administrative duties forestalled closer involvement in play: "when they're doing free play, we're not spending as much time as we could [with them]" [S2.8].

As well, Sonia found she had so much to plan that she would squeeze out time for this while the morning children played.

> We've got so many things to plan that sometimes, which is not good but it's necessary, you're taking time away from the kids in the morning to get a few things done while it's nice and quiet. [S2.7]

> Now if during free play, if I have everything set up, if I'm ready for the day, then I can go and play. Or I can watch or I can do anything. But, if otherwise, that's the time when I'm running around like a chicken with my head cut off, getting things ready. [S6.3]

Monitoring, supervising craft, maintenance and administrative duties, finishing up planning and preparation for future activities — all these prevented active attention to the observable play activity of the children. This practice during free play occurred in spite of or in contradiction to her valuing of play, her sensitivity to it as developmentally appropriate.

You know, I don't think I've had a chance to sit down in the block corner and play, with any of the kids, since I've gotten here. [S2.8]

I find that there is just so much to do — that we've always got one more thing. [S2.8]

But I don't think it's good to have to do things when they're there 'cause I can't — I'm not playing with them. I'm not really as attentive to them even if they want [me] to. [S6.4]

Here was a friction point where two valued priorities conflicted. In the face of the multiple agenda competing for her attention, play, in spite of its apparent value to her, was simply the least prioritized.

INCIPIENT MOMENTS OF DEVELOPMENTAL APPROPRIATENESS

Although her practice was primarily one of teacher dominion and Sonia did not attend to children's play, she nevertheless sounded very supportive of individual children's needs and interests in our interviews. And there were moments during my visits when she offered individually tailored support to specific children. It was sometime into my analysis before I understood that these moments always occurred with individuals, within a broader script for a specific time frame: they had the status of moments of a developmental awareness inserted within the overall allegiance to teacher dominion and were both somewhat infrequent and atypical. For instance, there were occasional moments when Sonia followed the child's lead in child-initiated activity. Once Beth wanted to "read" to Sonia, and did so with Sonia prompting her with questions about the illustrations to help Beth construct a "text" [SF4.5]. Another time, Rachel sang "Jingle Bells" continuously while Sonia sat and listened, seemingly enraptured, with formidable patience [SV2]. I later commented that these did not seem to be typical events:

No! They weren't typical events. Normally I'm not sitting down with the children to interact with them in this way. When I am sitting down, I am often feeling restless because I feel there are other things that "need" to be done. [Sper18]

Even as she sits she feels the pull back into the larger structure of all the things she must consider doing, as if this individual activity, while valuable, cannot be prioritized, is not quite fully validated.

Sonia followed a similar pattern in group contexts, too, in which, very occasionally, a child-initiated direction was followed and her agenda for the group interrupted, as in the instance in which Egbert was upset with the placement of the five snowmen's hats on the flannelgraph and Sonia invited him to come up and fix them. Another time in circle, everyone wanted to talk about skates, and it was, as Sonia, said, "way off base. And I was just tired and didn't feel like going off on skates [but she did]. I mean I try my best to go with them, because it's their circle" [S6.10]. Here we see the value of a child-centered concern overlaid upon a framework of teacher dominion. The sense that the circle is for the children, that it belongs to them and that their agenda matters, is very much present, though in general, Sonia's circles were teacher-directed with teacher-selected content. Developmentally appropriate practice was an atypical pattern of resolution to dilemmas of choice within a dominant pattern of teacher dominion.

One place where her awareness of developmental needs went beyond the individual was in craft. Sonia was unconcerned with the product of craft, although she generally began with one in mind: "I think the process they're going through, what they're doing, is a lot more important than what comes out on the paper" [S3.6]. With the shapes theme, for example, she offered sponge painting, the sponges cut into geometric shapes. She described this to me as a time to "have a chance to talk to them about what they [shapes] are, and see what they know" [S3.2]. At the end of the session, all the papers were a solid, unvaried, muddy blue-gray, as the children enjoyed spreading the paint with the sponges, rather than printing. This did not bother her, even when her co-worker said teasingly, "Where are all your shapes, Sonia?"

Her care for children and her willingness to accept them as they were, her implicit awareness of developmental appropriateness, was thus present and brought to the forefront of practice at moments when no other pressing need arose out of the teacher-centered scripts she felt she had to keep in place or out of the very real constraints enmeshed with her practice.

CONSTRAINTS IN SONIA'S PRACTICE

Throughout our interviews Sonia's talk was peppered with references to problems, constraints in her work. Although her setting was well equipped and well designed and she could ask for things and they would eventually appear, it was clear that she suffered many more difficulties than the others with whom I worked. These difficulties can be summarized as an intensification of work through a multiple agenda and time pressures that were not manageable as well as a loss of control over her work processes.

When Sonia talked about time, it was as if it was a pressure cooker into which she was constantly trying to squeeze one more thing: "there's so much to do that we've always got one more thing" [S2.8]. Trying to squeeze more into the available time than would fit or at the cost of something else was a continuous theme in the contexts of planning, carrying out program, getting bulletin boards rearranged, managing to get a complete lunch break. If, for example, she got the dishes done quickly, she would get her full hour for lunch [S1.4]. There was never enough time to plan—2 hours once every 2 weeks, but she planned for three groups a day. Thus she accomplished some of this while the children played or "you might be able to stick it in when you've got the primaries in the afternoon" [S1.11].

There was always a sense of harassment from the multiple agenda around Sonia. This was worst at noon, with the influx of 34 rowdy schoolchildren too big for the room. She conveyed this distress over lunch in such comments as "there's so much to be concerned about" [S1.5] and "I can't relax, . . . I can't relax anymore. So, it's kind of hard to relax with that many kids in the room and you know no one else is watching them" [S2.4]. She described lunch as her "insanity time" and "I've got a pounding headache" [S5.2]. "I'm really finding it's just too much" and "I think at lunch time it would be fair, a little bit fairer if they had two teachers here" [S1.5]. These comments were made from October through January. In May she said informally that she felt the noon hour to be unsafe because they could not adequately monitor all that was happening among so many children. As well, morning children whose parents were late picking them up would be caught in the melee: once, Alex, seated in the art area away from the others, stood up on his chair with scissors in his mouth to look toward the door for his father. Sonia dropped the spoon with which she was ladling soup and dashed over to him, asking him to color instead (because she couldn't monitor his use of scissors). The incident upset her: "it would have taken nothing for him to fall and those scissors go through his throat" [SF2.3].

After three in the afternoon, attendance was constantly on her mind, for she had to track children in and out of the setting over a 2-hour period and "it messes up our routine" [S2.20]. So much of her daily time was spent monitoring the revolving door, checking who was coming in and who leaving, and there was constant tension for her between this and trying to run a program with planned activities. As well, sometimes she would not know who would show up for her program, as in the after-lunch program for "primaries": "I saw him [a 3-year-old] walk in the door and I thought, oh no, there go my activities for the week" [S6.15]. He was too young for what she had planned, and her loss of control in not having an intact group of children with whom to work contributed to her sense of difficulty.

The times when the afterschoolers were present were particularly difficult. The noise level alone, with so many in a space designed for preschoolers, could make the room unbearable. The children plugged their ears, too, she told me, and it could get so "you can't function in the room" [S2.16]. She had to break up fights and excessive movement, and she coped by instituting a structured program of choices for different days. "When I think of a good day, it's when the afterschoolers don't drive me insane at lunchtime, and I come out without a headache at 5:30" [S6.13]. In addition to this, she was concerned with various administrative rules and worried about how she was doing. She was expected to provide a circle, craft, song circle, and movement time for each group; submit the plan book; change the bulletin board each week; do the attendance a certain way; and so forth. Under normal circumstances none of this might have proved too difficult, but considering the conditions of her work, the numbers of differently aged children flowing in and out during the day, and the type of program that she tried to provide for them, the result was a situation in which she simply could not accomplish what she intended. Here is an example of how the combined weight of multiple constraints and scripts for organizational procedure destroys program for children:

> Sonia is in the kitchen, a small room off the classroom, doing lunch dishes. There are 24 children in the classroom. It is noisy, but without much movement. Each child is in a place, though they may squeak, roll, set the chair legs on their feet, lean on their chins, and so forth. Iris is about to start a craft, and has newspapers spread on two tables and 11 children sitting waiting, when a parent arrives, insisting on seeing the director about a financial matter. No director. The parent talks to Iris for some time. The children wait, rolling, leaning, squeaking. Sonia is still in the kitchen. The parent absorbs Iris for 7 minutes, then goes off to the telephone. Iris approaches the tables of children. "Thanks for waiting so long." A child whines about the long wait. "I'm sorry. I had to speak to M's mother. I'm the only one out here; Sonia's doing dishes. I'd appreciate it if you'd be patient." She sounds tense and harassed. [SF6.6]

Theoretically, Sonia could have stopped doing dishes to deal with the parent so the children would not be left waiting for activity. Theoretically, the colleague could have sent the parent to Sonia and spared herself the children's irritation and her own displeasure at their impatience. However, the force of practice as it is institutionally organized, the script in place, is so powerful that neither teacher could at that moment alter its direction to see a different possibility. This is in spite of the fact that, for Sonia, opportunities for the children to be active were considered very important [S2.4, S5.2]. Yet there were many situations where this valuing of activity was overridden by some event, like this one, that preempted activity. It is clear that time pressure to accomplish set tasks renders a teacher almost unable to see any other agenda but the task.

Sonia coped with a tightening web of constraints and scripted patterns of action in several ways. In May, when we discussed her feedback paper, she said she was using simpler themes with a wider appeal (such as eggs, buses, and milk rather than "children at work around the world"); she wrote less in her plan book because she found it unnecessary to write so much; and she had let the bulletin boards go.

SONIA'S SHOCK AT THE FEEDBACK PAPER

As Sonia and I discussed aspects of her feedback paper in the final interview, it gradually became clear that she was astonished at the discrepancy between how her practice appeared to an outsider and what she thought she was doing. She recognized my description as accurate but was appalled because this was not how she thought of herself. There was uncomfortable tension for her around the revelation of how her work appeared (on the basis of what she said and did) and how she thought it appeared. This took several forms. One was the realization that she was highly programmatic in practice when she valued spontaneity and, to my total surprise in this interview, showed a longing for a spontaneous, dynamic approach:

> When I was reading about it, first I thought it sounds so rigid. I sound like this horrible beast who's got this thing, this book [planning book] there, and the kids have to do everything . . .
> *Have I overstated it?*
> No. I guess when I look at it, I seem so much more structured than I want to be or think I am? And yet you've got examples where I look back and I think, well that's how I am! And that's how I do things. But that's not how I want to be! [S7.14]

She went on to describe how she would much prefer to be spontaneous, to follow what the child wants to do in a group, for instance, but that she does not know how to do this:

I'm not spontaneous enough, probably because I don't feel comfortable enough to go off into that area [topic child raises]. Because I don't know what I'm doing! You know, it's foreign. And that's where my plan comes in. At least, the plan, I know what I'm doing. But when you move off, you get scared. [S7.14]

But where do you learn to do that? You don't. It's supposed to be spontaneous. . . . So how do you make yourself do things that you think should be done? I think I should be going that way, but I don't know how to! [S7.14]

Here she argues for the value of an ability to follow the child's lead, a value that is part of the model of developmental appropriateness, and she sees herself, through the feedback paper, as doing the opposite most of the time. Clearly Sonia is unfamiliar with the planning and observation of children that would permit her to notice, extend, and support ideas that emerge from the children, and just as clearly, these are aspects of practice that she implicitly values and occasionally uses, although she cannot yet see how to integrate them fully into her practice.

Sonia's reaction, in reading her feedback paper, was traumatic, as she valued the idea of beginning with the child and saw, in contrast, how her highly programmatic approach covered up much of what might emerge from children. She acknowledged that she did not address children's needs and interests in preparing activities, that it was not part of her practice: "not really, ideally I'd love to say yes, but not really" [S7.18]. Nevertheless, the tension for her arising between her allegiance to teacher-dominion and her awareness of a developmental approach, different from the one she used, was apparent in the reflection and self-criticism in her responses. One senses, below, that she was appalled that she was not carrying this out more extensively in her practice. "But no, not really. [Then said with irony.] 'Start with the child and work outwards.' No, we don't do that! We do whatever's easiest. God help me" [S7.17]. In this honest and almost bitter self-appraisal lies something that needs to be acknowledged. It is neither easy nor necessarily possible to construct the practice one values and hopes to enact as teacher. A particular belief may not be part of performance skills just because a teacher wants it to be. A teacher may value an aspect of developmentally appropriate practice, may even think she has the theoretical understanding that underpins it — there sits Sonia's 4-year degree — and be quite unable to perform the scripts it requires. In Sonia's case I argue it was the combination of the weight of an overwhelming multiple agenda — an inexorable web of constraints — and a practice deeply embedded in scripts for teacher dominion that ultimately all but buried a valued aspect of her practical knowledge.

The consequences for Sonia of this combination of a choking web of constraints, deeply embedded teacher-centered practice, and inattention to children's play emerged toward the end of the year, when Sonia's comments at our final interview indicated that she had fallen into a pattern of quasi-custodial care of the children, with most of her attention drawn away from them to other matters.

> I'm not really involved in their play, I'm always somewhere else. . . . I feel that I was hired to direct a room and move kids around and chairs and tables and make it look nice, and what I actually should be able to do is work with the kids . . . 75% of my time is spent doing the little things . . . when I think that 95% of the time should be spent with the kids and 5% the little things. . . . I feel like I'm not needed, and it's a bad way to feel, because I think they do need us, and Iris and I have been so wrapped up in things about this job . . . where you notice that as soon as you sit down at a table, all these kids come over and sit by you. It's like they're craving some teacher attention, and not getting it. And that was really scary for me. [S7.16]

The job she mentions is elsewhere. When in April an out-of-province school board swept into the area looking for 200 new teachers, Sonia and Iris were among the early applicants. The consequences of abandoning play for Sonia were that she realized she was not mindfully present for the children. When she saw this, it startled her, because it went against what she believed she should be doing.

Sonia left day care work at the end of the year — got the job with that school board. It would be unfair to argue that she left merely because of particular work processes, yet it is fair to say that it was not a situation that she wished to repeat, and the quotes from her data set show that the stress from her work brought her close to a physical breaking point. It is also fair to say that staff turnover is a considerable concern in day care. In the United States, the rate is higher only for the occupation of gas station attendant (Galinsky, 1989), and in 1984 it was 30% (Jorde-Bloom, 1986). Sonia's experience of noon and afterschool hours with its hectic multiple agenda, and her evident sense of surviving rather than coping (apparent in the physical symptoms suffered), demonstrates how an expanding multiple agenda becomes aversive and, in combination with other factors, contributes to destroying the very practice the teacher values and hopes to construct.

4 | Shifting Allegiances

An advantage of returning to revisit teachers some months after the initial cycle of visits and observation is that the process of incipient change becomes visible in retrospect. This chapter is a story of change, changes that were not visible or open to articulation until some months after the initial visits.

When I began working with Nora in late November, she was 3 months into a new job in a day care center, after 5 years as assistant in a private setting. In the day care center she worked with one colleague, Danine, an experienced teacher, and together they cared for 14 children between the ages of 2 and 5. When I asked Nora the following June about the most significant thing in her background, she said it was changing jobs: "I would never have lasted in the field if I hadn't switched" [N6.12]. She described her former work setting as "highly structured" (fitting descriptions of teacher dominion) and found her new situation quite different. Nora had graduated from a 10-month program of intensive training in early childhood education after high school.

During the research project, nine of the children Nora and Danine cared for were boys, most hovering around their third birthday, and two of the girls were 2-year-olds. The effect of the age distribution was that most of the children functioned as very young 3-year-olds, with several older children clearly not fitting this pattern. In her room, Nora was always quiet and calm, emoting a slow-moving ease and comfort around children.

Her room was high-ceilinged, with a high loft in one corner, a table area to one side, and dramatic play and block areas on the other. She often sat on the loft stairs or on a chair watching the children as they played. Once when I was filming the block area in free play, tiny Rose, in floppy hat and high heels, wandered in from the adjacent housekeeping area. Nora asked her to return to housekeeping, worrying she would trip over the blocks in her heels, but when Rose said, "I want to smile for the lady," Nora "just left her," later describing this to me, amazed at the child's awareness [N5.14].

There were no burdensome constraints affecting Nora's work during our time together. Sometimes the adjacent toddlers encroached on her program (a smelly diaper wafting through story time, for instance), and she had some difficulties with fire drills and with handling student teachers, but she had a single group of children and control of the work space with her colleague.

OVERVIEW OF NORA'S PROGRAM

Nora began her outline of her day in the same time-oriented fashion as Jill and Sonia. "It's free play until 9:30, between 9 and 9:30 everyone has gone to the bathroom, 9:30 is tidy-up time" [N1.1]. However, the routine that her colleague, Danine, had adopted was more relaxed than the school-like design of time, with fewer scheduled activities and a more flexible approach toward altering those that were scheduled. In concert with this, the program focus of Nora's colleague was on making changes to the environment to encourage more desired activity on the part of the children. Nora adjusted to this different handling of time as part of her adjustment to a new position, and she told me this center was "less structured" than her previous work setting, though she had not realized it until she experienced working here. Just as she had previously adapted to a school-like routine, Nora adapted to this relaxed handling of time and said she now preferred it. Experiencing a different construction of time allowed her to make the comparison and to value one over the other: she no longer took for granted that day care time was like school time. When she was faced with a relocation to a room she feared was more rigid in its use of time, she resisted this. "I worked there in the summer for a couple of days. It was very . . . routine. You know, like right to the time. And like here we're really flexible with it" [N5.3].

For a new worker, adjusting to the time schedule is a priority of successful functioning; she is no help to her co-worker if she cannot quickly understand and replicate the schedule. As a taken-for-granted basis for functioning, it does not have to be thought about and can be carried out automatically, as a shared script for action, for practice, and becomes important as part of the mutual cooperation valued by staff.

Because Nora was in a work setting new to her, she was inheriting scripts already in place in the setting, some of which were new to her and some, familiar. These new scripts involved this more relaxed use of time and a different form of program planning. Danine planned "curriculum webs," a broad topic used to generate ideas for a month's activities; as well, these were thought out in terms of changes that they could make in different play areas in the room, rather than as content for teacher-taught group times (Corwin, Hein, & Levin, 1976; Levin, 1986). Nora enjoyed rearranging areas, trying to determine what would draw children to activity under the loft (such as a typewriter and office supplies, or a bedroom for housekeeping), and compared this with not being permitted to alter materials in her previous job. Her colleague focused Nora's attention more on areas of the room and children's activity than on teacher direction, and her valuing of play was clear.

All the teachers with whom I worked believed that play provided children with important learning for their development. All mentioned learning to share, socializing, language development, and role-play opportunities as important gains from play. Nora commented as follows:

> They learn how to share. They learn a lot of language, a lot of role playing . . . just a lot, their basic skill of picking things up, you know, hand–eye coordination, all that kind of stuff is what they're learning from play. Cooperation. [N3.7]

> Like I think through playing that they're learning a lot more than if we sat down and said, "this is a such a such shape, show me where it goes." [N4.10]

Here she contrasts play with instruction, valuing play and implicitly the way conceptual learning is embedded within it. She did not instruct the children in teacher-centered episodes as did Sonia and Jill; rather, she read stories or sang songs in group times. She watched the children a lot and let children initiate interaction with her.

Closing Areas as a Script for Correction

However, there were patterns around resource management in her setting that she quickly adopted and that I characterize as scripts for teacher dominion. These were scripts for closing play areas and for corrections of children in play. To call these scripts teacher-dominated is perhaps unfair to teacher-centered practice, but I have not found a better term: the scripts imposed adult authority on children's play such that play was closed down, children did as adults said, and it was clear the adult held the power to determine activity. Such scripts were general and depersonalized, institutional in character, with the teacher fulfilling a role in carrying them out. As well, they were static, in that no real change resulted beyond the mechanical stopping of activity. The next day it happened again.

Three of the teachers I worked with—Nora, Carla, and Sonia—had patterns of closing off play areas from use during free play. This produced particular effects on the children's play. In both Nora's and Carla's settings, the table area of the room, sand and water play at its edges, was always open, but there were several areas that were frequently closed during play so that children were not permitted access to them. In Nora's setting these were housekeeping, blocks, and the loft. On my first two visits, both housekeeping and the loft were closed to activity; on my fourth visit, blocks and the loft were closed. All areas were open on my third and fifth visits. The loft was closed because Nora and Danine were not pleased with its functioning and were trying to work out its problems. Housekeeping and blocks were closed because of perceived "misuse" by children — they did not clean up or use materials "properly." To provide a sense of the dynamic enacted out each time this script was called into play, we will look at the boys playing firefighters after a visit from local firemen.

> Four boys play firefighters in the block area, each holding a quadruple unit block in his arms like a firehose. Part of their play pattern involved falling on the floor. Several boys jammed their fingers between block and rug in falling, pinching them. Nora instructs them "not to use the blocks as firemen, just to build with them. We'll try again tomorrow."
>
> "Okay, Julien, let's put them away, 'cause people are hurting their hands with them."
>
> "I want to build," says the child. He clearly does not wish to give up these blocks, pinched fingers or not.
>
> "Well build then."
>
> The four boys build lackadaisically, moving several blocks in a grid on the rug for a few turns of the hand, then are up and away with the blocks in arms as firehoses. Nora corrects them a third time: "They are for building today."
>
> "Oh, no!" says a boy, as he lays down the block. The tone conveys his displeasure at not being able to continue as he wishes, a tone of annoyance and of losing out. They build sporadically, and within moments the blocks are up in arms again.
>
> "Chris, this block needs to stay on the floor." A breath later, "Two more minutes and it's tidy up time" [NF3.2–3].

Nora commented that she found this play fairly "rough" and was afraid that

> They're going to get hurt, if they're not careful. We've explained to them if they're going to use them as firehoses, they have to keep them

in their hand. If they fall on the floor, their fingers are going to get jammed, other people's toes are going to get hurt. So if they're fire-hoses, they need to be in your hand, and if not, then they need to be built with. . . . But if we find that after a couple of times telling them, if it's not going to work, we'll just tell them to put them away. The next day, it's tried again. [N4.11]

There were half a dozen contexts in which this script was repeatedly used to handle correction situations. The block area was closed for "piling" blocks, rather than building with them [N1.6], the loft because children became excited and waved, housekeeping because the children did not tidy up satisfactorily. Once Nora surfaced a problem, she reminded children of "correct" use of the material. If this was ineffective, she closed the material or area for the current time period and said, "we'll try again tomorrow." This meant they could use the material tomorrow and she would assess whether they were using it "correctly," as she specified. If not, it was closed again. This script for correction was, in its impact on children's use of the room, the single most powerful and significant script for handling a problem with materials.

The script was a little like cutting butter with an axe. Nor was it connected to the teachers' belief in the value of play for development (this, in part, is why I call it teacher-dominated — the script arises out of a different framework for action), and when criteria for developmentally appropriate practice ask if materials are accessible, teachers say yes because they are in the room and do not think about how such scripts close off possibilities for using materials (Wien, 1991).

The consequences of such a script for the children are fairly obvious — loss of play space and material; truncation of play scenarios; having to find something else to do; loss of self-esteem and opportunities to develop their own personal scripts, memory, and language; and loss of personal power. But I argue that this specific script, used so frequently, had inadvertent consequences for Nora, too.

Why Nora Could Not Play

Nora could not play, she said, because the children rejected her presence. She stayed out of their way — cleaning, tidying, or watching — unless it was to correct children or add or remove materials. When I asked her if this was what she believed teachers should be doing, she quickly replied:

No, I would prefer to sit with someone and play with them. You know, like sit at the table when they're painting or something. These

guys, a lot of them, will just tell you, go away or not bother them.
[N3.11]

Although preferring to participate, Nora found that these children rejected her approaches. With a laugh, she said, "they find that I'm a nuisance" [N2.13]. She might go into housekeeping if a child invited her for
"a cup of tea" [N2.13], or she might draw the boys some roads, but
generally, "you try and stay out of it as much as you can and let them
play" [N2.13]. How did she herself describe what she does as the children
play?

> I usually just kinda hang around. [laughs] It's just standing around
> watching them or tidying up or putting things away — over Christ-
> mas was a perfect example. I went into housekeeping? And they told
> me to get out! *Told* me to get out. I was not allowed to play. I was
> surprised: they told me to get out. [N3.5–6]

Nora was seen by the children as an inhibitor of play, something
intuitively recognized by the little boy who said "Oh, no!" when she
wanted the boys to build with the blocks rather than play firefighter.
Because the children saw Nora as a rule-maker, one who frequently shut
down their play and removed them from play areas, their instructions to
her to leave the play area were a way to ensure the survival of their play.
Here we see the effects of such correction not only upon the children, but
the inadvertent outcome of the tactic for the teacher. It left her marginal-
ized, sitting on the loft stairs watching. But that's not the end of the story.

THE PROCESS OF CHANGE IN NORA'S PRACTICAL KNOWLEDGE

Nora was one of four teachers who were drawn alternately between two
frameworks for action, teacher dominion and developmental appropriateness. However, while Jill, Carla, and Sonia tolerated the conflicts and the
tensions that arose from them, Nora, by the time of our final interview,
indicated she had clearly made an allegiance to one framework. She was
thus conscious of points of change in her work and in herself as a teacher,
compared to when I first observed and videotaped her.

These were pivot points for Nora, places where Nora saw that she
could take a different direction from the one she had previously used.
Again and again throughout the June interview, she remarked as we
talked, "that's where I've changed a lot."

In our final talk, there were eight points of change that Nora consciously raised, and two of these were general or sweeping changes that would clearly affect everything else she did. These two major shifts in mental set included a new awareness of a professional attitude, expressed as a conscious attempt to remain consistently positive with children:

> I'm trying to be positive, and [pause] trying to be positive in like trying to be consistent; every day being positive and not being negative or grouchy or down, because it does affect the children. [N6.7]

Second, she was conscious of a change in her thinking, a shift from a teacher-centered approach toward a more child-centered approach:

> And thinking more about the children than worrying about if they're learning their colors or their shapes. But worrying about if the children are having fun playing, or what *they* want to do, instead of what I want. So that's the biggest change I've found in myself was — worrying about what *they* want instead of what I want. [N6.10]

Changes in Nora's Conception of Crafts

I have selected one of the eight areas, the development of her concept of craft, to show in detail the evolution of one particular change. At our first interview in November, Nora spontaneously offered me information on crafts while telling me she now had nine boys and this made her work more difficult:

> But a lot harder, because they're not interested in craft time. The boys just aren't interested. It's harder to get something that they're interested in. It has to be something that's messy and quick. [N1.2]

All fall, she had offered teacher-prepared crafts for children to glue together. Basically she considered two parts, such as a paper plate and tissue, or cutout feathers and crayons, and she began with the idea that the children would produce a specific object such as turkey feathers or pumpkins. And at this point in time, there was considerable tension, for the young boys did not want to do these crafts.

Nora's definition of a successful activity was as follows:

> If the children are happy with it. If they are laughing and enjoy it and say, can I do another one, can I do another one, then it's successful. If no one shows up, like I've had [happen], then I call it unsuccessful and try again. [N1.18]

At our second interview a month later, she was seeking explanations for the children's lack of interest in her crafts:

> But that's what I've found so far, anything that's going to take them more than a minute or two, they're not interested. I don't know if it's because of the age. We only have four that are 4-year-olds; the rest are younger. Some of them are just going to turn 3 this month, next month, so I don't know if it's the age with them, or if it's because they're boys. [N2.9]

She was looking for external explanations for the lack of success, explanations outside the crafts themselves, which she saw as exemplary. Yet she was troubled and had found herself changing the crafts slightly to accommodate the children.

> I found I'm doing these quick activities because other activities they don't want to do? They only want to do something that's quick. . . . Like there are some Christmas crafts that you could do that might take a little bit of time. They're not interested. They want to do something that's quick and they can go. Something that's quick, put it on the [Christmas] tree, and go play something else. [N2.8]

> I said to my co-worker, I've never been so disappointed in my crafts in all my life. And I think it's just because they're different children. We have more boys and they're definitely not interested . . . they just want to play in the sand [and with] blocks. [N2.19]

Her disappointment was exacerbated by the fact that she spent considerable time, by her account, in preparing these crafts.

There was thus enormous tension between her personal criteria for success and the children's reaction to her crafts. It nettled her all fall, but her sole change to the activities had been to reduce their scope, to make them shorter, quicker, so that they required less investment of energy, concentration, or commitment from the children. This reduction of the activity was the first step in the change process.

In January, she had discovered, perhaps by chance, that teacher participation in an activity drew children's notice.

> I set up ice cubes and paint and we were painting with ice cubes so I sat down at the table and did it. Three people came over to me. Now if I had just set it up and left, no one would have come. That's the

only way we can get them involved is to do it [with them], and let them come on their own. [N3.12]

Because she generally was not involved in the activity of the children, either to participate or converse about it with a child, this occasion marked a change in her normal pattern of actions, a change toward more teacher interaction with material, and then she saw how it drew the children, this watching of the action possibilities that devolved from her hands.

Experience in Generating Ideas

At the next interview, Nora discussed changes that she and her colleague were making to the room. There was enthusiasm, vigor, and excitement in her voice:

> Move the easel back down where the sandbox is? . . . and put the art things back and see if that will attract them again to go and take what they want to do. And how can we change it [the environment] to make it more exciting. Which is really hard because where I worked before we never changed a thing: the shelves were the same for the 5 years I was there. [N4.16]

Suddenly, in the fifth month of work in a new setting, she saw herself as starting to think more about ideas to try out in the room, changes to materials, to areas of play. In her former workplace, she felt she could not do this. Here she has discovered that she has a chance to be active, to have ideas and to try them out, to suggest, for instance, a music corner, an idea that Danine supported. "Your mind is constantly going, thinking about different things [to do]. . . . Like before I would not even bother to think about it, and now it's [her brain] really starting to think" [N4.16]. Nora experienced for the first time what it is like to have ideas that she can try out on the environment. She was excited and moved by her activity as a teacher for, on this job, she had permission from her colleague to have ideas and take action. She was becoming more active as an agent interacting with materials herself.

Changes to the environment became a frequent topic of conversation for us. Within a few weeks, the art area was all reorganized and there were plans for a new shelf. "I said to Danine, I said, 'they play with the same toys. Can't we make it a little bit more exciting, you know, and maybe we'll get some different people doing different things'" [N5.5]. Now she wanted to pass on the excitement she was feeling about her own work in the environment to the children, wanted to see them doing some different things that they didn't do before. Suddenly she was interested in novelty and variety. (Thus far, she had not thought in terms of what she could do in interaction with the children, but only of what she could do to the room. One might argue she did not see herself as a potential source of knowledge for the children, in spite of her use of scripts for teacher dominion.)

A few weeks later, it was Valentine's Day and Nora was disturbed that her new student teacher had used most of the 200 wallpaper hearts Nora had prepared for craft. But it was the effect on the children that bothered her the most.

> I find it's a turn-off. I find the children don't use their own thinking. They copy what the other students are doing.
>
> So yesterday, the student showed Brie, well we'll do it this way, and put them [tissue bits] on the end of the pencil and showed her how. That was fine for Brie, but the other little ones couldn't do it, so they got frustrated . . . [Alexa] just walked away. That upset me because I worked hard cutting out my part. [N5.7–8]

Here she expressed her positive view of children's own thinking, their own way of doing something, and her dislike of the student teacher's demonstrating something that children then copy. She wanted children to use their own ideas. This was a major shift away from the point she had made in our first interview about tolerating children's doing a craft their own way. This was the first time she expressed the sense that the ideas of the children were more important than her ideas or the student teacher's ideas.

Perhaps after the very positive experience of being able to generate ideas herself in making changes to the room, her disposition toward children's ideas had shifted. She viewed them more positively. She had experienced what it is like to have one's own ideas accepted (not simply tolerated) and even encouraged. Thus the student teacher's behavior annoyed her because it imposed on children, rather than leaving them free to participate in the activity, but she did not quite know what to do about it, except to ask her to refrain from doing the activity in front of the children.

Recognition of Child-Initiated Activity

As well, when I asked Nora what she was thinking about as we watched her on the video sitting apart from the children's activity, seemingly uninvolved, she said: "When I'm sitting there I'm wondering why Rose is putting on her hearts and taking them off. And rubbing the glue with tissue paper. She said she was cleaning it" [N5.8]. Here she showed awareness of the child's process with the materials, certainly a process she did not plan for or think of, but she noted it, wondered about it, and let it happen undisturbed. She was thinking more about what the child was doing than about what *she* wanted her to do.

> If they're not going to do it my way, then that's fine. That's the way they want to do it. I think that's where I've changed a lot. This little girl painted her hand, and I just let her. Normally I would have said, "no, please paint the paper." And I just let her paint her hand. She painted her hand and she painted the other side of her hand and I was watching her and she painted between her fingers and then she said, "I'm finished," and she put her hand print on the paper and went and washed her hand. Before I would have jumped in. I've learned to sit back and relax! And see what's going to happen. And if it's going to affect another child, then I would step in. But she was hurting no one. [N6.14]

This is a remarkable shift toward permitting child-initiated activity that formerly would have been vigorously corrected.

By June, the general shift toward the tolerance of child-initiated processes of which she speaks extended to her planning for crafts. She told me how appalled she now was at some of the things she had formerly done:

> I stopped with the precut stuff. I stopped that. I was looking at some of their artwork on the wall, like after you're out of the room you go back in, you think, did I really do that?
>
> When you're outside the room and you look in, you think, oh I couldn't have done that [in a whisper]. So I've stopped. . . . You can use twigs to glue and stuff like that other than precut things. Or put paper out and let *them* cut. [Put out] the wallpaper and let them cut out what they want. That way I've changed a lot. . . .
>
> Yeah, I've changed a lot. . . . Thinking I had to put the children first, instead of what I want out of an activity, I have to put the children first. And before I wasn't. I was thinking what I wanted out of the activity. What the finished product should have been. [N6.19]

Not only could she describe concretely how she had changed, giving me examples such as the child whom she permitted to paint the skin of her hand, but she could see her previous beliefs in the context of this change and tell me the difference. The difference was that now she was watching children, observing them for the process that interests them, whereas formerly she was embedded in a process that focused on mastery of teacher-prescribed content in a teacher-centered way. Once she could see the difference in these approaches, particularly in the context of crafts, she wondered aloud why she had been like that. "And then I stopped and I was looking at the room thinking, I didn't do those things. And it was like, why? Was it the easy way out?" [N6.18] With this comment — "was it the easy way out" — Nora tacitly acknowledged a major difficulty for those wishing to construct developmentally appropriate practice: it must be done *against* the inclination to perpetuate the scripts in place in the setting, against the tendency, present in many day care settings, to follow the teacher-centered practice previously constructed.

The Dynamic of the Process of Change

How did Nora herself account for these changes in mental framework, her conscious shift from practice strongly modeled on teacher dominion toward more child-centered, developmentally appropriate practice? I extracted half a dozen reasons from our interview. Their accumulation operated as a salient intervention that disturbed her previous understanding of practice and allowed her to construct a different image. First, she had switched jobs from a position where she felt she had been kept static to a center where teachers used less teacher-centered practice than in her previous job [N4.16]. She found her new co-worker a valuable model, seeing how her positive approach to children worked. As well, in the 3 months between my last visit and our final interview, she had been temporarily moved to another group and had also substituted in other locations for some weeks. As a result of these shifts in locations, she saw various other approaches and broadened her awareness of possibilities for practice. This particularly affected her view of her previous crafts, as just described.

The above-mentioned aspects were an external impetus to change. Change cannot occur without internal impetus as well.

> Just stopping to think about what I was doing, you know. Like I would never go home stressed out or frustrated, but I would go home and think, *why did I do that?* You know, you go home and you think about the day and why did I do that? No wonder that child's having a hard time with me, or said that to me. Things like that. Just going home and thinking about the day and thinking oooh, I've got to stop jumping in. [N6.15]

Reflection, then, was one means by which this change occurred for Nora, as she described the normal process of reviewing what she had done after it happened — and then critically examined what she had done that she did not like.

She also attributed some of the change to her participation in the research project, saying it had helped her considerably. She said the questions I asked increased her reflection: "It was just like a guideline to think" [N6.23].

What was abundantly clear was that Nora had surfaced the teacher-centered practice in her work as problematic and was consciously attempting to change her image and her practice. This she clearly told me as she identified herself as having followed teacher-centered practice, but saw herself as shifting to emphasize play.

> I found I was this way for a long time [using teacher-direction] . . . like when I first started work in September, but I find my way has gone a lot to the play group models. . . . I find, well, like I was [doing] shapes, colors, and stuff like that, because it was drilled in my mind for 5 years. . . . [With play] I've seen it working in the rooms and that's what I've been turning to, because I find I'm more comfortable with it. [N6.9]

> I've been trying to get out of the school model thing. [N6.10]

> And thinking more about the children than worrying about if they're learning their colors or their shapes. But worrying about if the children are having fun playing, or what *they* want to do, instead of what I want. So that's the biggest change I've found in myself . . . worrying about what *they* want instead of what I want. [N6.10]

This general shift to thinking more in terms of what the children are doing and wanting to do, rather than what the teacher might want, is a significant step in the direction of a child-centered approach. In Nora's case, the change in her scripts for craft — away from specific predesigned products toward an interest in child-initiated processes with materials — was set within the broader spectrum of changes affecting all aspects of her practical knowledge.

And in our final interview, she told me, in passing, that she and Danine were trying to find a way to stop closing blocks and housekeeping:

> [We] have tried to work out a way where you don't close anything. Instead of closing something we might redirect the child to something else, or sit with them and try, you know, to work the problem out. [N6.1–2]

She continued that "this is the way it was when she went in the room" [N6.2]; in other words, Danine had inherited a particular script for correction when *she* began work in the setting. Now they are thinking about it together, searching for other solutions.

What we see in Nora's case is the power of the scripts already in place in a setting to prescribe future practice. The practice in place tends to be perpetuated, I argue, out of the immediate need, in day care, for the new worker to adjust to the routine that is in progress when she enters the setting: she is no help to anyone if she cannot sustain it. And because routine practice so quickly becomes automatic, these scripts become taken for granted as natural, normal, expected, as a given that is essentially unchangeable.

It may take enormous reserves of energy and flexibility of mental set to address these powerful scripts, to question them and begin to generate alternatives. That Nora and Danine could do this says much for both of them, as well as for the administration that ensured a setting not overburdened with constraints: it was possible for them to think about what they were doing.

5 | Tacit, Invisible Practice

The most experienced teacher with whom I worked was also the teacher whose practice was most difficult to surface as something for discussion: parts of her practice were inaccessible. To ask a teacher about the structure of her program, what holds it together, is not a question that she does not know: she performs the complex scripts that form the bedrock of repeated practice every day and knows this intimately. But for Carla, such questions did not make sense. We got along very well, and her program was considered very effective by those around her, but we disagreed in our view of her practice. I have an unfair advantage in reporting this, but you will hear her response to my feedback paper and my resolution of this, and you may compare this interpretation with your own sense of the situation. And when, 4 years after the original research, I gave Carla a draft of this chapter (as I did for all the teachers), there were points with which she disagreed, and we met for two hours discussing her comments. I have revised the chapter to include these, indicating in the text where this is the case. My argument is that Carla's practice was one of teacher dominion. Carla's argument was that this was not so, but that play and a developmental approach were favored.

Hers was a crowded center, overflowing with children, many at risk of poverty and its consequences. The director told me they had found that "middle-class methods" did not work with these children and only produced chaos, whereas someone "who came on like a sergeant-major" was much more effective. She meant by this that individual redirection was ineffective, that the behavior of the entire group had to be addressed in a way that showed strong leadership, for she found that the children required a clear sense of who was in charge in order to respond to adults in focused ways. In this she echoed Delpit's argument (cited in Stipek, 1993) that African American children, accustomed to an authoritarian style of parenting, "expect an authority figure to act with authority" (p. 35). The center's concern connects directly with the broad questions occurring in the literature asking whether developmentally appropriate practice as currently described is sufficient for children at economic and educational risk (Bredekamp & Rosegrant, 1992; Mallory & New, 1994; Reifel, 1993).

Carla had a firm rein on the room, but she also granted children more freedom from the rein than the other teachers in the classroom. "I find [in] this center, some children are very rough. Very rough. I worked with children in another day care and I never saw children that rough. This is a challenge for me" [C4.13]. Carla worked with 9 preschoolers in the morning, with 22 5-year-olds added in from noon until 5:30. The mornings were relaxed and calm. The noon hour was suddenly hectic with the press of 31 children in the room. At 1:15 some returned to school (different ones every day, because they go back only two days a week in first year), and these returned at 3:15. Parents began to arrive around 4:00, but many children were still present at 5:00.

She had two colleagues, and when all 31 children were present, they usually divided the children into three groups. Carla took 9 to 11 children, the older and more difficult ones: her 13 years of experience established her as a veteran in day care. Carla has an undergraduate degree in economics and completed training in early childhood education in a 2-year extension program in a community college setting.

CONSTRAINTS IN CARLA'S PRACTICE

Carla, like Sonia, was harassed by being unable to accomplish what she perceived had to be done within a certain time frame. One day she looked out the window at close to five o'clock and realized she had not yet moved the center van, which she drove on field trips, to its correct location. She left the room, still full of children and staff, muttering, "Too many things to do" [CF3.6]! Another time, in watching the videotape, she noticed that she still had her boots on an hour after arriving back from a field trip: she had not had time to take them off [C3.18].

Both Sonia and Carla coped with large numbers of children at various periods during the day (at peak times Carla had 31 and Sonia, 34). In both settings there was simply so much happening (except during group activities) that it was extremely taxing, no matter how many adults were present, for the teacher to manage to keep track of events in the room. Carla's multiple agenda after school included monitoring the play of 31 children, dealing with the arrival of parents, checking the pick-up person against her list of who was permitted to take the child, checking two attendance lists, correcting children who choked or pushed or punched in free play, receiving messages from the director, and somehow also attending to the children taking direction from her at the craft table [C5.12]. On one occasion I remarked that she seemed to be doing two things at once: "not two things, lot of things!" [C5.12]. With her years of experience, she coped with aplomb and did not like my suggestion of a harassing multiple agenda. But I saw the major constraint for Carla as an intensification of work processes resulting from high numbers, a tight schedule, and rowdy children: there was simply a lot to manage, but as she said, "I can handle it."

OVERVIEW OF CARLA'S PROGRAM

Carla's center, too, used a school-like design of time for its program, the schedule especially tight in the early afternoons because they provided a series of outings for the children—to the library, the swimming pool, the skating rink—which they believed many children would otherwise not experience. In their program there were two principal and contrasting segments, teacher-centered group activity and free play. The teacher-centered groups used themes, the same sort that Sonia and Jill used—abstract concepts of shapes, colors, alphabet, and numerals, which were changed weekly.

Carla provided more content and activities than is often the case with a stereotyped use of weekly themes. For instance, when the theme of the week was "Smell," the interest table was crowded with small jars of cosmetics and lotions, the water play area abounded in smelly bubbles, milk for snack was flavored with peppermint, and the craft was the making of enormous tissue flowers, huge and bright as peony heads and profusely sprayed with perfume: these went out of the room, homeward bound, like flags of radiance. This provision of interesting material was coupled with a high valuing of children's play in her talk with me, and—appearing to contradict this—a favoring of teacher dominion in practice, as suggested by the following examples.

During the theme on smell, Carla had prepared a guessing game with foil-covered jars, each containing a strongly scented item—vanilla, after-shave lotion, lemon, and so forth. Its purpose was to see if the children were familiar with the smells and could identify them correctly, "and it's kind of fun, you know" [C5.4]. She presented this in a large circle and passed each smelling jar one at a time, from child to child, inviting them to guess its contents and pass it on. The children who did not have a jar in hand waited their turn. This took considerable time, but, with the exception of two restless older boys, the children awaited their moment with the jar intently. On this occasion, she stopped the game after doing four smells, as this had lasted 30 minutes while each of nine children took the jar in turn; she stopped it because she did not want them to sit longer—it was 4:05 and they had been sitting close to an hour after school.

I could have done [the entire tray of smelling jars, about 12] but I didn't want to because they were restless because they just came from school, right? . . . I thought I would stop because I didn't want to sit longer and longer. [C5.7]

During my five visits with Carla, group times during which the children sat largely inactive, waiting and listening, occupied roughly 50% of the time between 9:30 and noon, and between 3:00 and 5:00. The children were 4- and 5-years old.

If the teacher engages in teacher-centered activity, she controls the single legitimate activity and has but one agenda; as long as she can delight or coerce the children into following it, she solves her monitoring problems. In fact, an implicit benefit of teacher dominion is that it keeps children quiet and eases the teacher's need to monitor when such a large group is present. It is legitimate to ask whether more teacher-directed activity occurred in part because it reduced the stress of monitoring, a major constraint for Carla.

Another arena of teacher-centered activity was Carla's craft times. These were not a source of ambivalence for her as they were for Jill and Sonia. She required children to follow her instructions precisely.

During free play, Carla sits at the art table, three or four places for children around her, and children may choose to come or not, as they wish. Arthur winds around the table several times, as if assessing whether he will join, as several other children manipulate paint-coated strings. Carla helps Arthur into a smock. Standing, he picks up a string from a central tray and, holding it high, wiggles his hand so the string descends on top of the paper in coils.

"You fold the paper," Carla says.

"Yeah, yeah, I know," he says confidently.

"Here," she says and takes the string from his hand and lays it down the middle of the paper, folds the paper in half over it, demonstrating the technique she has in mind. Arthur pulls the string out from between the folded paper and opens it to see the result. [CF2.2, CV 1]

As we watched this on the videotape, Carla said:

He is not following the direction. . . . He knows how to do that but, on purpose, he's not doing the, pulling through the paper, pull[ing] on string. Eventually he will do it, but he has a tendency, like if you say something, he always says 'No!' Right away. And he wants to do [something] completely different. So in day care what we are trying to do, we don't want to give in, like if you say something, you stick to that point. Like okay, you are told to do that, you do it. Sometimes we do the free art, like they can do anything they like to . . . [and] sometimes we direct, like this is the things, we want you to use this, this, and this.

So here you wanted him to do the process that you've shown them?

Yeah. [C2:12,13]

When Carla read the draft of this chapter, she reminded me that because this child had a history of aggression toward other children, she anticipated that he might "swing the string around—get somebody" and intervened to keep his attention focused on the activity, and that all children were not so closely instructed. But what I saw as an observer was a child genuinely interested in the movement of falling string and its pattern on paper: I did not understand why this was not a legitimate part of the activity. She, with her rich experience with this child, saw something else: what we have here are different readings of his intention. Some of her craft activities were "freer" (conversation, June 1994), and some were to be carried out according to the sequence she specified. In the latter, actions initiated by the child that were not seen as part of the planned process were deflected or redirected to fit her plan.

Because Carla showed a strong preference for a play emphasis in her talk with me, but also kept children attentive to long discussion circles, I probed her relative valuing of these—free play and teacher-directed times. She told me that they learn "in both situations" but that they don't enjoy discussion "that much," especially after a day in school. I asked her why she felt she needed to do the discussion with them rather than let them play. Carla responded: "Well this goes with the theme. They have to know what the theme is for the week" [C6.37]. Why were themes so important to Carla? She believed that the government department that licenses day care required them, that they "had to be done." This was not in fact the case.[1] Nor is Carla alone in holding this myth of practice: I have heard it many times in many settings in our region.

Such a myth is a story or script about how one should behave: it

---

1. Day care is regulated at the provincial level in Canada. The staff of Day Care Services reiterated that they accept a variety of program approaches—themes, curriculum webs, Montessori, Waldorf, High/Scope, and so forth—and require documentation to indicate that some program is being offered. This is apparent both from their written guidelines (Nova Scotia Department of Community Services, 1990) and from Jane Grantmyre, Supervisor, in personal conversation, February 1991.

prescribes performance. Jorde-Bloom (1986) points out that what people believe to be true influences practice, not objective fact, and Hatton (1987) believes these images of how one should behave shape practice as much as experience. Seefeldt and Barbour (1988) observe that teachers often perceive a mandate where none exists. Believing weekly themes were required is one such myth, common where this study was conducted. In accepting this belief, Carla shows herself to be part of her social setting. But she loved children's play and could not yet see that her theme content was embedded more naturally in their play through some of her activities, in ways that had more meaning for them, than it was in discussion circles.

Held in tandem with this strong emphasis on teacher dominion was Carla's belief in the efficacy of play. Carla told me emphatically, "children's play is learning, like playing they're learning everything" [C5.16]. As an example, she described how a child might learn that he cannot mold dry sand, "so they have to put some water to make it moist, and they can make a shape out of it: children's play is learning, they learn through play" [C5.16]. Her view reflects the conventional discourse about play that has developed throughout this century, moving in the direction of increased acceptance of children's play as valuable to development.

While Carla seldom joined the children's play, as did Liz and, in some contexts, Jill, she constantly observed it, assessing materials she could add or remove: most of the color and liveliness in the room came from the materials she added to activities, such as the elaborate cosmetics table during the "Smell" theme, which sparked long, involved play.

But teacher dominion — the teacher as the one in control of who does what — was also in place during free play, for this center, like Nora's and Sonia's, had patterns of closing off certain areas during play time. During three of my five visits to Carla, housekeeping and water play were closed, and on two visits the block area was closed during free play. This produced a variety of consequences.

The first and most obvious was that the children needed to check with a teacher whether an area was "open" before entering it. The area did not look any different: it was simply unoccupied.

"Are we allowed in blocks?"
    "Yes, it's open." [CF3.3]

"Can we go in the house?"
    "The house is not open yet." [CF1.10]

Thus the children could not assume that the play areas of the room were available to them.

The other major effect of closing off areas was that Carla and the staff acted as gatekeepers to the major play areas. There were several other factors that contributed to this teacher role: one was the crowded nature of the room (31 children in a space with minimal square footage), and another was the limits on the numbers of children permitted in each play area. This produced a competition for play spaces among the children.

When previously closed areas were opened up again, there was a "rush" on them. These popular areas for play were suddenly sought out with some intensity. The pattern that emerged was that particular children would extract a promise from Carla that they could use an area when it was reopened. Then other children had to negotiate their entrance contingent upon these first-comers. In my five visits, I found 2 dozen examples of this gatekeeping function. Two examples demonstrate this gatekeeping and its effect on specific children.

When water play is reopened, five children rush pell-mell to occupy the three spaces. Two girls quickly take up spots, and Bertram throws himself into a shopping bag smock, sliding it up over his legs and torso, and quickly positions himself. Beth is too slow getting on a smock and disconsolately leaves for the art table, where she takes out paper and colored pencils. She looks sad.

George, who also came too late to play here, waits for a space, chatting with others or with me, his eye frequently on the tub, waiting for a spot to open up. Carla stands, arms crossed, beside the water play area, watching but not interacting. George sees Carla fiddling with the sleeves of Dana, who plays in the water, pushing them up under the shopping bag handles on her shoulders.

"Oh, she's coming out! I better hurry!" George runs to line up at the tub, apparently thinking Carla was helping Dana take off her smock, since this is a service she often provides for the children. However, she is simply pushing up the sleeves of Dana's sweatshirt to keep them dry. False alarm. George returns to a chair near me, takes up a pink pencil and tiny scrap of paper, and makes several marks, eye on the tub. After 30 minutes of waiting, he went again to stand by the water play tub. At this point, Carla invited him to wash out a margarine tub of red paint in the bathroom down the hall. He went happily. [CF2.1–6]

In our interview, Carla told me the three girls had asked for water play earlier, as it was being closed, and she had promised it to them: "'I'm closing it down and later on when you finish [art] you can play,' so I kept my promise." When George came by half an hour later, she told me she had said to him:

> "You're just standing there. Why don't you do something while you're waiting?" And he just stood there. "Okay, would you like to help me?" And he said "yes." "Why don't you wash this pan?" and he was happy to do that. . . . Two things he can do, water play plus wash the container. [C2.15]

She also promised him he could be first in water play after lunch, and said that she would inform the other teachers, which she did.

Here is another instance when the same child, whom Carla noted had difficulty settling down to anything, negotiated a play space in the housekeeping area. Three children were allowed in housekeeping. Two girls had just been asked to leave, and a third remained.

> George asks Carla, "Can I go in the house?"
> "I've already promised Elijah and Janet. When they come, you have to leave, okay? Do you want to do it that way?"
> He nods, goes off to the area. Shortly after, Elijah and Janet arrived, and George was told to come out. I sit close to the entrance. As he passes me he mutters, "I didn't get to stay in there very long." I say, oh, maybe he'll get a turn some other time.
> "I don't think so." [CF1.11, 16]

A sense of competition for desired resources—scarce resources, from this child's perspective—is very evident, and one senses his belief (momentary perhaps) that they won't easily be accessible to him. The room was, in fact, well equipped, and Carla told me they could generally acquire whatever they needed [C5.18, C3.19].

What is difficult for the outsider to see is that this dynamic structure, produced by the intersection of several strategies for coping with numbers and providing program, could not have been better designed to convey to children that while there are interesting things to do in the world, and some people get to do them, it may be difficult to gain access to them. The hidden curriculum in this program matches the grim economic reality that the families of these children struggle with daily. These children learn early that resources are scarce. This was an inadvertent outcome of practice, not recognized by staff but powerful in its impact on individual children. It flies against the staff goal, evident in the busy program of outings, to provide more for these children.

Thus a frequent part of gaining access to play areas was eliciting the teacher's help, for, otherwise, a child might decide what he wanted to do and then find no room at the inn. Part of Carla's gatekeeping function, then, was determining the order in which children would play in particular areas. Teacher dominion in opening and closing areas and in allocating specific play spaces to children was a major feature of free play in her setting.

The other common strategy was the removal of a child from an area for actions that the teacher perceived as undesirable. In this example, the correction was so fast, as the teacher anticipated a potential problem, that nothing was said by the children.

> Some intensity is present among the four boys in the block area, the beginnings of intent discussion — passion — about something. How can I tell? The way they are turned to each other, eyes alert, something passing from one hand to another, the sharp watchful eyes of the others. An increase in energy. There has been no noise, no fighting. It is primarily nonverbal. Carla tells Wayne to leave the block area. Wayne cleans up immediately and leaves. [CF5.3]

Carla told me, "He was aiming the knightrider car; the other boy was just lying down and looking at him, and he was just aiming right at his face" [C6.6]. She asked him to leave because she anticipated that he was going to hurt someone. (The child previously hurt someone so badly he required stitches across the nose.) I asked her if she felt the strategy worked. She paused for sometime before responding. "Yeah, it works. [considering voice] . . . ah, a difficult question, does it work. That time it works, they stop doing that. Then they'll do it again" [C6.8]. She gives me an example, how with Bertram she is continuously correcting him for being unable to stand in line: "he's wibbling, pushing people, and poking, elbowing and saying 'oh, I didn't mean to'" [C6.8]. He is removed from the line, given time-out, knowing Carla is "licked off" [sic] because she has to "stay back" with him. Next time, he says "'I'll be good, I'll be good,' and he stays for a few seconds, then he goes again knocking people, jumping again" [C6.9]. It is clear that removing a child from a context is a last-resort script for action that does not have sufficient impact to keep the child from repeating the actions that led to the correction. Whatever the problem, removing the child is a temporary solution. Contrasting with this interpretation of mine, however, is Carla's comment (June 1994) about Bertram: "he improved a lot by following the routine; we have to have discipline for this day care."

DEVELOPMENTAL APPROPRIATENESS AS ATYPICAL PRACTICE

Because Carla's practice seemed to me deeply split between teacher dominion and an allegiance to developmentally appropriate play, I made a
specific search of her data set for pivot points. Here is one that shows how
teachers can struggle with the conflict of deciding whether practice should
tip in the direction of developmental appropriateness or teacher dominion:

> Around 4:30 I always wanted to do something really structured, like
> reading a book, everybody listen, or storytelling, like maybe I have a
> record, they can listen to it, like Robert Munsch and all those
> things — they always like it. But then you think about [it] again — oh,
> well, those children can play with so many things, why [do] they
> have to listen? . . . I feel guilty when they can play free play.
> [C4.19]

Here we see the clash between two values, the importance of play and of
teacher-centered activity. Carla saw these as mutually exclusive, that is,
only one could occur in a specific time frame. This is a pivot point where
she considered another way of acting and rejected it in favor of play. The
possibility that both could be offered at the same time was outside her
frame of reference at that time. That fact, though, is interesting, because
it is precisely how craft activities were always offered in her setting, with
the children free to choose the teacher-directed craft as a choice during
free play. In June 1994, she could imagine them occurring simultaneously,
"if there is a room [for the story]."

Carla and I disagreed about her practice. In reading descriptions of
her circles and crafts, she thought the feedback paper made it sound so
strict, severe, when she felt it really was not so [CF6.1]. In our interviews,
I had been puzzled by contradictions between her talk and her practice.
In our first interview, she told me themes weren't obligatory: "we don't
force them — 'You cannot do anything else, this is the time we're doing the
theme' — we don't do that" [C1.14]. She meant, of course, during free
play, but it was exactly what was done during long compulsory group
times: every time I visited I saw her conduct a whole-group activity in
teacher-centered fashion for 30 to 60 minutes. Or "We really don't close
[play areas] altogether, it's all open" [C1.16], when I frequently saw
areas closed for a variety of reasons. When I described my impression
of group activities as long and focused on listening skills and following
instructions, she countered with examples of circles that were not like
that — a theme on tools and machines with a visiting carpenter, a time

when they made milk shakes [C6.29, C6.32]. This discrepancy between her view and my view was bothering me as I sought out pivot points, and I began to see a parallel between how some dilemmas or possible tension points demonstrated patterns of typical and atypical resolution, as suggested by Berlak and Berlak (1981). I found five such instances in her data set and report two here to provide a sense of them.

Carla's normal script for bathroom routines was to take her group of 9 to 11 children all at once at specified times. The bathroom was a bit of a walk, and she could not monitor it from her room. However, she also occasionally used the practice of permitting children to go one at a time by themselves. Two, she said, would make an enormous mess, squirting water to the ceiling, climbing on the sink or toilet top, but one at a time could be trusted [C1.9]. She liked to do this sometimes because, as she said:

> I like to see their freedom, and a little bit [of] responsibilities, and a little bit of trust. Sometimes I make [an] exception; I let them pour their own milk sometimes, . . . and go to the washroom, and they really like that. [C1.10]

Now the situation becomes clearer. Her typical practice reflects teacher dominion, the teacher in control. The occasional practice reflected a more developmentally appropriate approach, favoring the child as individual and values of self-responsibility and trust. She told me she was the only teacher in her group to offer the children this. We see in this atypical practice a thread of developmentally appropriate practice inserted within an established set of teacher-centered processes and offered as an occasional event.

Here is an explanation for the contradictions between us. When asked about things, she frequently described the atypical pattern—whether because she valued it more or thought I valued it more, or some combination of these factors—and I, in observing, was witnessing the more typical patterns of practice.

Another instance occurred when she provided rocks for the children to paint red at the craft table. Her typical practice in free play was to control access to resources: here she limited the number of rocks for each child to three, so everyone would have the same quantity to paint. However, two children enjoyed this activity so much that they asked to paint more. She gave them each one more rock.

> Remember, I said I don't give any limitation? [But] if they paint too many I don't have enough rocks for them [afternoon children]. I did

not want to stop and say, "no, you cannot do that," because if they want to do some art, I should supply [it]. [C2.11]

This instance shows her typical practice—careful control of access to resources during free play—and an exception (though still controlled) that she made to support further activity. Again, we see an atypical pattern inserted within a more frequently used pattern. The atypical pattern is more reflective of developmentally appropriate practice—valuing self-motivation on the part of the children and her obligation as a teacher to provide activity when children seek it.

Although tolerance of two conflicting frameworks for action never surfaced for Carla in the same way as for Sonia or Jill, what I saw, nevertheless, through this particular sieving of her data, was the implicit wish, the desire, the will, to be incorporating developmentally appropriate practice—and its appearance in her practice as an atypical solution to dilemmas involving individual children. Her response to George's attempt to gain a water play spot can be seen in this light, too: once his need for water play was apparent to her, she invented an individual solution that provided for his need. She sent him to the bathroom with a paint pot to wash out, commenting to me that he gets a bit of responsibility and some water play, as well [C2.16].

What we see is the tendency for developmental appropriateness to be inserted into present practice as an atypical pattern. Thus, if the teacher is asked whether she uses a particular practice reflecting developmental appropriateness, as happened when we discussed a criteria representing developmentally appropriate practice, she of course honestly replies that she does, and gives examples. The fact that this occurs as atypical practice within another framework for action may or may not be problematic for her: it is the outsider who initially may find her talk and practice contradictory, until this broader interpretation is understood.

When these moments of developmentally appropriate practice occur, because they address the needs of the individual child, they do not affect the overall structure or the dominant patterns of practice in the setting. Moreover, the fact that proponents of developmentally appropriate practice think of it as prescriptive of overall structure is simply not recognized in such situations. The ideology of developmentally appropriate practice focuses on individual development and prioritizes the individual in the teacher's thinking. Thus the overall structures that it implies as dominant patterns of practice may not be at all apparent to teachers caught in another framework.

The desire to identify with developmentally appropriate practice, with its overarching value of honoring children's intentions in play, may be the first step in altering practice. First, there may be a predilection to open up practice at chosen moments to make room for content and needs emerging from children, as with George standing beside water play.

The teacher-centered practice that Carla implemented so thoroughly remained, I argue, largely tacit, invisible practice, so taken for granted as what must be done that the frameworks for providing interesting things to do for children were never questioned, even with probing. Nor was the contradiction between this and her wish to provide play opportunities visible.

Perhaps it is difficult to see in part because the ideology of developmentally appropriate practice focuses on the individual child and his or her development. If favors individual rights and thus reduces the importance of social organization, the handling of life in the group (Wien, 1991). Those of us who propose developmentally appropriate practice could be more explicit about the scripts for functioning as a social group in this practice, so that teachers are not left functioning in scripts for teacher dominion that are inappropriate to the practice.

When Carla read this draft chapter, she had several concerns, some of which have been embedded above, but for her sake I wish to clarify a further point here. She wished that her work as a member of a team was more apparent, that her colleagues were more present, that the fact that the system of "rules and routines" was shared, and not hers alone, was played up. She thought it sounded as if one person was responsible for everything when she was "just following the routine."

> But the rules — the block area not open, housekeeping not open — those are the rules, we are just following them.
> *Could you change the rules?*
> Well, you could, but in 5 minutes, they are going to lunch, or school, so you couldn't change the rule, you don't have the time.
> (June 1994 conversation)

For me, her concerns illustrate one of the terrible difficulties of creating text intended to mirror a context — it cannot do so exactly, of course, because lived life is so much more complex than what can be written in the space of a chapter. One tries to do it justice, telling the story that relates to one's argument and recognizing the limits of the vehicle of communication. Because my focus in the original research was developmentally appropriate practice and difficulties for teachers in constructing it, my case descriptions may not show how this social reality is constructed by all its members and how permeable [the term is Dyson's (1993)] we are as individuals to the beliefs and values of others. Carla is quite right that it was a shared responsibility, a shared structure within which she worked: it is also clear that her attempts to provide the practice she valued explicitly — that favoring a more developmental approach — went beyond that of other staff in her room at that time.

6 An Image of Developmentally Appropriate Practice

Of the five teachers with whom I worked, one described what she tried to do as developmentally appropriate practice [L6.15]. Liz had a clear allegiance to a single framework for action and had spent the previous year altering her practice to reflect this. When she suffered tensions it was between her image of practice and the reality before her. Liz was in her ninth year of work when she joined the research project. She had just completed a 16-month in-service training program (in High/Scope) several months prior to this, so that we come into her room when she was consolidating new scripts for action, after undergoing major change in thinking out how to construct her practice. Until she began the in-service program, she used the patterns I describe as teacher dominion. By her own admission, when she started in day care work at age 19, she saw herself as a babysitter, one who changed diapers and took children for walks [L6.19]. She now conveys a strong sense of herself as a professional person, an advocate for young children, with a very different view of what she should provide for them than she previously held.

Liz cared for 15 children 2 to 4 years of age and had one co-worker, Bess, a novice. Many families in her center suffered economic difficulties—unemployment and welfare, for example—and, as with Carla, many of her children displayed low tolerance for frustration; she had to anticipate outbreaks of kicking, swearing, or temper tantrums. As with Carla, her group included several challenging children: one boy when angry would spin around the room with lightning speed, whipping everything off the open shelves until an adult reached him.

Liz is a talker, full of vitality, earthy, tolerant of mess, always finding room for one more child on her lap. She said the significant things in her background had been the totality of her training (she graduated originally from a 10-month intensive program in early childhood education), extending from the distant past through her present, and the fact that she came from a very large family: a person who grew up as the ninth of 10 children, she retains a strong empathy for individual needs in the midst of a multitude.

Her room was large and high-ceilinged, with many areas and a split-level deck, including an area for pets with fish, gerbils, and a guinea pig. During activity times, the floor was strewn with materials. The room had a slightly run-down, lived-in feeling. At each of my visits the environment had been changed—housekeeping moved up to the loft, or the central area rearranged to open it up, or a planning board with photographs of areas of the room to facilitate choices, or a big new easel added.

Liz was not bound by a school-like time frame as the organization of her day. When I asked each teacher to describe her work day, the others began with time and its breakdown. Liz began with what she was trying to accomplish with the children and a description of the room.

> We want to follow the plan, do, review, so that children are looking at what they're going to be doing, then they're doing it, and then we say, "This is what you did." So they're making a lot of decisions on their own, which I feel is really important for them to do at an early age, and they're really in control of their own play. [L1.20]

This is a radically different conception from that of the other teachers. She prioritizes not the time structure but the goals of a specific framework. In particular, offering choices and continuous opportunities for interaction with materials were important to her, and, as we will see, she had worked out ways to include these curriculum goals in routine matters such as serving lunch and using the bathroom.

Nor was her reaction to routine tasks similar to those of the others. Two teachers, Liz and Sonia, were expected to wash lunch dishes for their group. Liz and her partner did not wish to take time from the children, reducing staff at the busiest time of the day [L1.18], by absorbing one person in dishes after lunch, so they worked out a scenario in which they placed all the dishes in a large bucket in the classroom to soak, and washed them at 5:00 when there were only a few remaining children. "They love to go to Esmeralda's kitchen and sit in her chair and have a cracker and get the dishes done" [L1.18–19]. Doing the dishes thus became a special time in the day, a change of pace and location at a time when teacher and children could accomplish the task in a relaxed way.

Her in-service program had legitimized the value of prioritizing the children's development (and thus their activity). This permitted Liz to see a conflict between her image of practice and reality. Having seen the conflict, she had worked out a solution that met both the need to get the dishes done in accordance with health requirements, and the desire to provide the children with more adult attention (two staff, instead of one) at the busiest time of the day.

During the period of the research project the major constraints that Liz absorbed and coped with concerned several demanding children with special needs and student teachers, whom she found often did not understand her practice and might undermine it. Once, for instance, a student refused a difficult child another slice of fruit from the snack tray: he got mad and upset the tray onto the floor. The student's refusal was inconsistent with Liz's practice, which was to offer choices where choice was possible, and Liz knew the stressed little boy was expecting a choice of fruit. Since she had, in fact, several challenging children, there was an intensification of work from the demands of those children interacting with the need to introduce several student teachers to her practice.

THE TEACHER'S AGENDA

To describe Liz's program, I first outline what emerged in analysis as the teacher's agenda, what she does in the setting. Since this was not based on the organization of time, I present it as an outline of scripts for action that she used as she worked, actions that encapsulated her values in practice.

Here is how Liz described the key characteristics of developmentally appropriate practice:

> It's child-oriented: it's not teacher-directed, teacher-controlled. It's child-oriented and -directed, you know. And it's not like a laissez-faire chaotic thing, I hope not — sometimes it is — but in general, it's child-geared. I feel it meets their needs. It's for their development. It's Piaget-based. I believe . . . It's *fun!* They're children, it's fun! I like that. [L6.14]

In all contexts of the day, whether during routines or in free play or outdoor activity or while baking a cake with a small group of children, Liz was attempting to provide the children with choices and with "positive experiences" in which they could initiate action, control their own activity. She believes that this will encourage the development of independence and self-esteem in children. The limit to their activity is that it be constructive, that "they're not hurting themselves or the things in the room, or other people" [L1.20]. She began with observation of this child-initiated process and surrounded this with language and other strategies to support the children's attempts to be active agents interacting with their environment.

The focus for programming is "basically around the child's interests" [L3.2] and meeting children's needs in play. One week, carpenters installed a toddler-sized set of stairs to the loft, "and the children, the whole rest of the day, everything they picked up was a hammer, so we brought out hammers and we brought out wood . . . and they got into all kinds of other things with building and construction and wearing hats; that was stuff they showed an interest in" [L3.2]. Her framework for action thus focuses on observing children's interests and providing for these.

As a teacher, she is actively involved in the activity of the children. When asked how she spends most of her time, she said, "playing with the kids, I hope, yeah, playing with the kids" [L3.21], or "down and dirty" [L1.4], which is how she described to parents the direct quality of her involvement in children's play. A year ago, she told me, she could not have said this, for she was using much more teacher-centered practice, and the difference is both the in-service training and her new co-worker.

In Liz's work, play and program are integrated, occurring together. In other words, the teacher's agenda for activity is to match her responses to the agenda for activity generated by the children in play. I asked if there are any differences between the two, play and program: "Gosh, I hope they go side by side, I hope we're meeting their needs in play" [L5.7]. The following sections describe how she has built her values into the scripts for action that are part of her newly established practical knowledge.

Routines as Vehicles for Choices

Liz believes that children should be offered frequent choices across all contexts of her setting, even the most mundane routines. Choices and child pace were built into all daily maintenance routines, such as lunch, bathroom, and "tidy up." Children did not wait in line to go to the bathroom all at once but went in groups of three or four with a teacher. Liz commented about their procedures for handling bathroom routines:

> It's very smooth, it is very smooth, and it gives — you know, some children want to brush their teeth for a very long time, and look in the mirror, and it gives them all that time they need to do that. [L1.16]

Lunch was arranged in small bowls with child-sized serving spoons so that children could serve themselves small amounts of beef stew and coleslaw, and thus could actively estimate the match between their appetite and the amount they put on the plate, quickly learning to assess what they could eat. Morning snack was generally fruit, cut into a multitude of small segments, and again they could choose as many slices as they could eat, so they had the experience of making decisions about this. When a student teacher prevented a child from taking one of each kind of fruit at snack, Liz told me she corrected her later, saying:

> "It was okay that he wanted another orange. If you'd looked at his napkin, [you'd see he wanted] one of everything and that's all right. He could have 10 of everything, that's okay. That's the point in this classroom — choices. You know you can make the choice." [L2.17]

The routine maintenance aspects of the day were permeated with a sense of taking time, not rushing children, and of noticing their interests. Nowhere was this more obvious than in the daily "tidy-up" ritual after morning free play. Since materials did not have to be put away as they were used (and certainly the speed with which toddlers switch track from one activity to another helps account for the trail of previous choices across the floor), everything was gathered up all together in one giant "tidy up." This was done at a gentle pace so it could be enjoyed as activity, and children were invited to find interesting ways of accomplishing it. David used a hollow block, a triangle shape, as a bulldozer to try to push spilled cornmeal together for sweeping up, and when an apron from housekeeping turned up at the foot of the aquarium, Tina wore it up to the loft as a way of returning it. On my first visit, I was so impressed by the mess that I could not imagine how it could possibly be cleaned up: even as cornmeal was swept up it kept respilling. "Our goal is for it not to be a chore. It's a time where we can think of all kinds of different ways to put things away in our classroom, and there are lots of positive things happening there" [L1.22]. Tidy up lasted perhaps 15 to 20 minutes, with everyone involved and invited to find interesting ways to accomplish it. Amazingly enough, at each visit, the classroom was restored to order.

Observation as a Teacher Process

Much of Liz's talk with me, whatever the question or image on video, included her observations of children's interests, process, discoveries, behavior problems, or ideas. If her concept of program provided a framework, a set of lenses through which to see her work, the first step before taking action was to see, to perceive fully what was happening before her. All of this information was offered spontaneously, without my asking, in a kind of running commentary revealing her thinking and excitement or concern about the actions of individual children. Here is an example:

> And when we did this small-group activity, Lynn's in my group, and what she did for the full 20 minutes, was with a small measuring

spoon, she took one bean at a time and she filled up a medicine cup, and when it got full, she dumped it back into the big one really quick. It was like she wanted to keep doing it again. . . . I had more medicine cups; I said, "would you like [more]?" No, she just wanted to fill the one. And the whole 20 minutes she just enjoyed that so much. [L2.4]

Out of the flood of observations, some things are selected to act upon. In the next section I describe the quality of her interactions with the children and the scripts for action that I saw when I analyzed her data set.

Support of Child-Initiated Activity, Interests, and Ideas

As noted, Liz wanted to support children's choices in their play, their ideas and processes in activity. In her interactions with the children she displayed many broad scripts for action to support their activity. There were at least nine that I observed or found in our talk together. I have illustrated them here with one or two examples, but these are all aspects of performance of practical knowledge that she used day to day.

Providing running commentary on children's actions. Perhaps the most obvious strategy was her use of language with the children. When Liz walked through the door, the energy level in the room palpably picked up, as she began a continuous flow of talk describing back to children what they were doing. They crowded around her: where Liz stops, interesting things are about to happen. "'I see you're putting your broom under the table, you're pulling it toward yourself,' and children love to hear what they're doing being described to them" [L2.9]. She believes that providing a running commentary of talk to these children is highly significant for the development of their language. Surrounding the actions of the child with talk is a theme in her personal theory as strong as the notion of choices and positive experiences. She did this shadowing of children, describing their actions, so much that she said she no longer thinks about doing it; it has become automatic [L2.9].

Participating in child-initiated activity. Liz joined the children in activity, doing it alongside them, and noted that wherever she goes, the children will follow, happy to be around an adult. Here is a description from fieldnotes:

At 9:35 Liz is at the planning board (an easel at floor level on which are arranged large color photographs of each area of the room). She is "on the phone" (a paper receiver), asking each child in the group around her what he or she is going to choose. David chooses sand, and when she asks what he will do there, he says "make soup." "Let's go make soup then," she says, and the entire crowd, Liz in the middle, moves over to the sand area to "make soup." Liz is as involved with the sand as the children, pouring and spooning and talking, asking Bobby what he needs to make soup—a bowl. Some children leave after a minute or two, but several stay more than ten minutes. [L3.2]

Demonstrating possible uses of material. Liz was constantly active with materials, trying out what the children were doing and offering other possibilities for action. A fragment of gym activity displays this:

In the gym, two boys take three galvinized steel garbage can lids from the storage area and bring them out onto the concrete floor. Liz sits down beside them, saying, "What can you do with these?" The boys grab multihued plastic bowling pins nearby on the floor and drum on the lids with them. The noise is piercing. They drum in short bursts, then stop. They smile at each other and at Liz, as if pleased and surprised to have produced such a thunderous sound. "That's loud, that's a loud sound," says Liz.

A tiny girl takes up a bowling pin and knocks it against the third garbage lid, alternating between loud bangs and very soft taps. Liz describes each sound to her—"That's loud; that's very soft"—as she produces it. Liz copies her sounds, alternating loud and soft, and then demonstrates a different quality of sound that she can make by drumming with a bowling pin on the concrete floor.

David stands up and lifts a lid in each hand and drops them clattering to the floor. They make a horrendous, electrifying clatter as they wobble rhythmically side to side until they stop. He continues this.

Bobby, watching David toss his lids onto the floor, picks up the third one and heaves it across the floor. Liz tells him, "Bobby, be very careful of the children when you're tossing them. He's holding it by the handle and dropping it." She demonstrates how to grip the handle and drop it directly down from his hand. He tries it as she demonstrated. [LF1.2]

Following children's lead. Often children want to do things that adults tend to restrict or not permit, such as banging on garbage can lids which make a horrendous noise. Liz did not restrict spontaneous activity that, in her view, did not hurt someone else. She noticed and commented on it. Of the noisy garbage can lids she said, "Anytime they want to bring them out, I let them bring them out" [L1.9].

One day Martin came with a fancy new child-sized umbrella that he wanted to show around. The children began to play with it, and Tina wanted to see it up. As we watched this on the video, Liz said, "He got it for his birthday and it wasn't that strong and I thought it might get broken—so I showed her how it would look up" [L3.17], and then she wanted Martin to put it safely in his locker.

When she put the umbrella up, clicked it open in its full position, and sat cross-legged underneath—Tina underneath it, too, staring up and shivering with pleasure—children began to run from close by to gather under the umbrella with them. The air was palpable with excitement as one more came, then another, and another, to see if they, too, could crowd under its open shelter. They stood very still, huddled together, almost breathless [LV3].

When we watched this on video, Liz saw it as an experience of inside versus outside, a moment of experiencing a boundary, and a moment of shared cooperative intention. "Everybody has the same goal. 'Let's get in' and everybody gets in. . . . And nobody had a problem, nobody was doing—'ah, don't touch me.' They also like the outside view" [L3.18]. If a child had something she wanted to try out, Liz would typically permit it, participating in the activity, too. (This is not to suggest she did not limit the children, for there were persistent, frequent corrections in this room that will be described later in this chapter.)

Asking and following up on open-ended, problem-solving questions. "What can you do with those?" Liz said of the garbage can lids, setting up the mental set that thinking up something to do with them is a fine thing. Exploration of materials is part of her vision of children's activity. Walter discovered that the garbage can lid made a huge indentation, a "print," when pressed onto a plush carpet sample. Walter forgot about the noise and began exploring this phenomenon. Liz noted at naptime back in the classroom that he was pushing his fingers into the rug (the same plush), and she commented to him, "You're thinking of when we were in the gym and you did that," and saw his face break into pleased assent [L1.10].

Here is another example from fieldnotes:

In tidy up Emma faced a sea of cornmeal and chickpeas in mounds on a table. "How could you get this off the table into the bucket?"

asked Liz. Emma picked up a child-sized dustpan on the floor nearby and made scooping gestures. Liz replied, "Yes, we can use that, that's a good idea. That's good thinking." [L2.10]

Here she invited the child to generate her own idea as a solution to a problem, and then applauded her success.

Interrupting own activity to acknowledge children's creations. Although she says it doesn't happen frequently, Liz will interrupt her activity with one child for something really important to another. Dryden one morning made a Lego construction and called in excitement to Liz to come see it. He said things like "whole boat go" and "make it big loud like this." As we watched this on video, Liz chuckled and added:

> This is very important to him, this boat he's made. The outboard motor snaps on, and when I started to move away, he's telling Bess that it's like his uncle's. And they go down to his land, so it's something that's really relevant to him. [L2.11]

Liz responded to his excitement by leaving the small group with which she was working at a table to go see what he had done and to talk about it with him. The motor boat was also displayed during recall at snack, so Dryden's production and his pleasure in it were twice acknowledged.

Extending children's interests. On the video, we saw Bobby carrying a small toy car and walking across to Liz, who sat on the floor. It looked like he was spilling something onto her lap.

> He's got cornstarch on the wheel of his car. And when he moves the wheel, it falls down on my pantleg. That's what he's showing me there. The flour [sic] falls off the wheel of the car. And I said something like "oh snow" and he said "yeah" and he went faster and faster. [L3.14]

Bobby was excitedly spinning the wheel, making it "snow" on her leg. Understanding his interest in the spinning action and the effect of the powder spurting off, Liz remembered she had a wooden water wheel, which she added to the sandbox for him.

> And he really enjoyed it. And he was talking about it moving, and when he poured it this way it went another way. I think I met his

need . . . Bobby was really intrigued, looking right into it, looking at how it all goes through. [L4.5]

There are numerous incidents like this throughout Liz's work day. The limit is not so much what is generated from the children, but the limits of the observation powers of the teacher to surface interesting processes to follow up.

Inviting children into areas; demonstrating and enhancing materials. This more general script intended for all the children may be carried out anytime, but is also a possible focus for a small-group activity. For instance, in November, Liz spent considerable time in the block area:

> so they really know there are animals and there are cars and there are many other different things. Often they go in there and play with the animals and cars, and the blocks never get touched. So we're showing them different ways, you know, "I can do this or that." That's starting to work, we're seeing little different things being used and used differently; that's nice. [L1.5]

Thus she actively demonstrated the materials that were there, and various possibilities for action with them, leaving the child free to pick up on this or to do something else.

Protecting children's ideas. One of Liz's most interesting scripts was active protection of children's incipient ideas, even if they could not articulate them. If there was a glimmer of intention, she would make room around the child, space for the idea to develop. This meant children were not asked to share materials and, in fact, were discouraged from infringing on material that another child had endowed with particular purpose. The effect was to leave the child who was about to infringe watchful and alert to Liz's explanations about what the child with the idea was doing.

> Sebastian stuck the end of a pink plastic skipping rope in a tiny hole in a low wooden wall in the gym and the other end of the rope in the hole of one of his tricycle's handlebar grips. Marcel started to pull out the rope from the wall hole. Liz stopped him, saying, "He has a special idea for the string. He's thinking about something. What's he going to do?" Liz asks Sebastian, "What does this do?"
> "It's a wire."
> Liz stays with him for several minutes, telling other children who encroach about his "wire." [LF1.8]

Whether this child had a clear intention (gas pump, for instance?) or simply saw two interesting similar holes into which to fit the rope, Liz was prepared to make room for his action as idea, give it space, presume intention.

> David built, with teacher assistance, a "train" of three plastic round stools, and identified a corner with, "That could be my land." Later he acquired a plastic riding toy train, which he put in the corner. Marcel spots the riding toy, empty, in the corner, and makes for it. David grabs it, struggles and complains in whines and shrieks. Liz explains to Marcel that David is "parking the train, that it's in the garage to be fixed," and says to David, "Do you want to tell Marcel about your other train?" Several children play on his train construction of plastic seats, which does not seem to bother him as the takeover of the riding toy does. [FL1.6,7]

Here, again, Liz protected the child's idea, not expecting him to share material on which he had imposed representation, but sharing the idea with other children, a form of acknowledgment of it.

I do not expect that this is an exhaustive account of Liz's scripts for action to support the child-initiated activity that she values, for her language and responses to the children were so varied, but it provides the flavor of her approach to carrying out her concept of play and program.

TEACHER PLANNING

In considering Liz's planning, I mention here both what she *does* plan and some conventional contexts for planning by day care teachers that were not of much concern to her. It is interesting to consider how Liz handled group activities, which are so frequently a focus for teacher preparation in day care. Circle time was merely a 15-minute transition between outdoor activity and lunch, its purpose to calm the children by channeling their energy into active games or songs, gradually bringing their activity level down so they were relaxed and could eat comfortably. Circle for Liz was "fairly spontaneous" [L6.14] and more probably active than quiet: "It's not necessarily a quiet time, our circles are not necessarily quiet, . . . and if children don't want to come to circle, they don't have to come" [L1.14].

Stories, often a focus of day care group activities, might occasionally be part of circle but were more typically read informally during free play, with three or four children huddled around Liz's lap and free to come and go. Neither her circles nor story times were contexts involving extensive planning: their character was more spontaneous. Nor was it obligatory that children participate in these. They were offered as activity choices within a context of other choices.

What, then, did she plan? Liz's planning focus was twofold. One aspect was changes to the room, to materials and areas to "enhance" functioning or to encourage children to "plan–do–review" in their play. The other aspect was planning for small group, occasions three times a week when Liz met with the same four children for shared activity. The expectation was that the children would be using materials extensively and interacting with Liz and one another as they did so. At the beginning of the year, Liz used these occasions to demonstrate areas of the room — the block area, for instance — showing possibilities in using materials and letting the children initiate their own actions. While she might use small-group time for something like baking a cake (a more teacher-directed activity because of the necessary sequence involved), she was more apt to pick up on some need or interest observed at free play and turn this into a focus for small group. Max, for example, hoarded a new puzzle that he especially liked, unable to tolerate the sight of anyone else using it, so Liz did a small-group time using puzzles.

> So when I was planning last week, I thought I'd better bring out lots and lots, tons of puzzles, and we'll try to have 12 puzzles and four children and there's lots of choices, and he was able to let someone else sit beside him and work on it and do another one. [L3.8]

My intention here is to show that children were always active in Liz's group activities, using materials and able to talk freely, and that her plans were based on observation of perceived needs. Their participation was not obligatory, although they generally wanted to do the activity that Liz was doing, but they always had one or two other choices, such as the book corner or sand area.

In her planning for program she was looking for individual children's needs or interests to address, or more general interests, if something caught the attention of a number of children.

> Now I'm not going to have 15 or 14 plans, obviously, but instead of what I've been doing the last 8, 9 years — you know, we're doing "Blue" this week, and we're doing "Winter" and "Transportation" and you know, blah, blah, blah, blah, boring, boring — we're trying to target in on their interests. [L4.2]

In focusing on children's needs and interests to plan what to do next, Liz utilizes both children's talk and children's actions as sources of ideas. Her response to the boy who inserted the skipping rope ends in the handle-grip hole of his bike and the hole in the wall shows how children's actions were seen as a source of intention. Below are examples of her planning responses, an example first of ideas as talk and then of ideas as action.

Ideas as Talk

Here Liz attempted to pick up on conversation during lunch.

> Jane was asking about elephants yesterday at lunch time. She had a cup that had a giraffe on it, and she said: "That's not like an elephant. An elephant has long things but it's not like that." She wanted to know what elephants eat. I said I believe they eat trees and grass. I found a book later on in the afternoon, and we looked at it, and that's what they eat. . . . And she wanted to be an elephant with the trunk, so we're doing little things like that. [L4.2]
>
> I think zoo animals might come into there, and I have sandpaper rubbings and zoo animals, all that. . . . They'll go in the sandbox, some'll go in the blocks, and they could go anywhere [from there, in the room]. [L4.3]

When she puts such materials out, it is a matter of seeing whether children's interest continues: there is no obligation to use them or to learn specifics about elephants or zoo animals.

Ideas as Action

Liz told me how popular Christmas was for the 2-year-olds in mid-January, that they were pretending to make Christmas things with play-dough.

> Christmas is very popular right now. I put all the Christmas cookie cutters away for playdough and I made playdough yesterday, and I took them all out again. It was really interesting, they were making trees and the lights were going on the trees and none of this conversation was going on before Christmas, none at all. And they were making presents and there was a bow on this present, and "that's my brother's name," and "that's my name," and "don't touch that one." It was really interesting. [L4.1]

In this case it was the materials to use in interaction with a malleable substance that allowed an interest shown by the children to develop a more elaborated form than she had previously seen. The important social experiences of children, whatever they are, can be expected to reveal themselves in their interests.

Thus, in her planning, Liz did not use themes or content that she had arbitrarily selected. She occasionally used a curriculum web, such as one at Christmas that drew on the customs of various families of different ethnicities (a Vietnamese family, a Mi'kMaq family) to broaden the children's awareness, but webs were exceptions. Generally, her intention was to stay close to what she saw emerging from the children's interaction with materials and people in the setting.

Perhaps most remarkable was Liz's ability to drop her plan in the face of more pressing needs or interests displayed by the children. She described how once in small group they used another room, where there was a turtle. She had planned to fingerpaint, but the children were interested in the turtle.

> *And they didn't want to fingerpaint? They wanted to look at the turtle?*
>
> "Teenage mutant ninja turtle," I said, but he wasn't a teenage mutant ninja turtle, you know. He looked different. So that was really positive, especially for John, who's [she picks up a piece of paper] — this is a teenage mutant ninja turtle. Everything is. This *is* a turtle. So whole small group we talked about this turtle, and we gave him something to eat, and it was really neat because he was up against the glass, and his face was all pushed up, so he was really close to us.
>
> *So you didn't do the fingerpainting?*
>
> No, they didn't want to; they wanted to talk about the turtle. And that was okay. And I think we did it [fingerpainting] that afternoon. [L6.26]

In other words, the intent of Liz's planning was the same as her overall framework: to provide positive experiences in which children have some control and lots of choices, to support child-initiated activity through observing the children's process, and to follow this lead with other possibilities that the adult can provide.

RESOURCE MANAGEMENT

In Liz's room all areas for play were always open and available to children, and all materials were accessible. "I really try and keep everything,

everything that they can reach they can use, as much as possible" [L3.18]. In fact, in her setting children clearly expected to interact actively with any material that entered the room. My video equipment was one example, and another was the record player, which Liz had to remove to an inaccessible height after it was broken a third time.

Materials could be moved about the room from one area to another; for instance, serving spoons would be brought down from housekeeping for use with playdough or sand. Liz told me that parents arriving before clean-up sometimes commented, "You guys had a rough morning?" Materials get dumped in the process of play, and "people say, 'what a mess.'" However, she does not see it as a mess, but as a classroom heavily used, one that has been played in for a very long time when tidy up is called.

Liz was one of two teachers among the five with whom I worked who kept all areas open and all materials accessible to children. As well, Liz always had messy materials available. She tolerated enormous mess and movement of children and stuffs (more than most of us could bear), bringing the room back to equilibrium with a mammoth tidy-up activity.

CORRECTION OF CHILDREN'S ACTIONS

Any correction of children takes one of two directions: it closes off or it opens up possibilities for action on the child's part. If it opens up possibilities for taking action, for child-initiated response, then the child's play can continue unbroken. If it closes off possibilities for action, then the child's activity is truncated, for the child has to find something else to do. A correction that stops spontaneous activity is a moment of fragmentation of development.

In Liz's case, corrections opened up possibilities for action. How did they do this? There are four important aspects that became clear in analyzing her corrections. Liz's corrections were *explicit, personal, particularized to context*, and *invited the child to do something*. They were explicit in that she used language that described what was immediately relevant to the situation: comments were concrete and descriptive, while explanations demonstrated relations between events. Her corrections were personal in that she addressed a child individually, frequently acknowledging his feeling or reaction in the situation, accepting that and working with it. Third, she dealt with the specifics of the particular context so that each correction was somewhat unique and particularized. Fourth, once the child had understood what he could not do, she offered other choices and asked the child what he was going to do. This last script gave control of action back to the child so that he could choose to do something appropriate within the range of what Liz found acceptable. Thus he displayed his competence and slipped back into active play. Here is a typical example, the event that sparked David's train construction mentioned earlier:

> Two boys struggle vigorously, both clutching a plastic riding toy, a train. Suddenly one takes off on it. Liz follows the boy on the train: "Look at this [she turns his chin toward her face]. I see an angry face. You really want it, but Gary chose it first. Let's go see if there's something else that could be a train." He gets off, the train is moved off by the other boy, and he and Liz view the room quickly.
>
> "What about the wagon?" "No." He spots a stack of three plastic tubular chairs, red, green, and orange, and carts the stack out to Liz. She separates them with difficulty, they are so stuck together. "That could be my land," he says of a corner.
>
> "Going to take your train in there?"
>
> He lines the three chairs one behind the other along one side, parallel to the wall, and sits on the first chair. Liz sits in the back. I hear "caboose." A student teacher comes and sits on the middle chair. "This is a great train ride," says Liz. [LF1.3,4]

The correction was explicit in that she pointed out that the train was already chosen by another child. It was personal in that she acknowledged the child's anger and the fact that he wanted the train himself. It was particularized in that the episode dealt entirely with finding an adequate train, the child's goal. Furthermore, Liz's comments invited the child to locate a satisfactory train. In the process of generating solutions — she offered one first, then he took the lead — the child solved the problem, that is, he satisfied his original goal, but in a new way. For Liz, this approach works; that is, it solves the conflict of the moment, but it also models problem solving and reduces conflicts among children as they begin to grapple with ideas for coping with conflict themselves. Liz's corrections were distinctive, and it was only in analysis of them that I saw that they included these four characteristics that I have described as qualities of explicitness, personalization, particularizing to context, and inviting the child to action.

Here is another way in which she "corrected" children, a move so subtle but so perfectly attuned to the children's intentions that actual conflict between children was forestalled. Two boys playing in housekeeping both wanted the same empty milk carton. As we watched this episode on video, Liz said:

> You can hear Gary, "I need some milk, I need some milk, I need some milk," and Dryden had the milk [the empty carton] and he was

using it. I can't remember how I solved that. I think I said to Dryden "maybe if you pour some milk in his cup" or something. [L5.3]

As we watched Gary and Dryden stand before each other for a long moment, Gary flexed his fingers over the milk carton, which Dryden warily clutched. Dryden paused and then carefully and slowly "poured" from the empty carton into Gary's "cup," his outstretched hand. Gary then turned away with his "milk." Where other teachers might have asked them to share or take turns with the carton, and some might even have asked them to leave the area, if each had struggled to gain the container, Liz saw the underlying intention and helped both children support it.

Liz demonstrated a willingness to observe children's intentions and to consider them honorable. Thus she did not correct children in situations where I as an observer recognized that some other teachers might easily correct. Her sense of judgment about both when to move in and how to react was tilted in favor of the child's intention. When a new child lifted the cover from the guinea pig's cage and gave it a poke, Liz showed him how to feed the animal through the screen at the side and saw to it that he attended Bess's small group, which cleaned the cage and held the guinea pig, thus helping him learn how to approach the animal [LF3.3, L3.7].

However, the ground rules in her room were frequently explicitly repeated, often with a personal comment or explanation attached, as when two children were more interested in a key chain than joining circle. "Ambrose and Ted," she said, "if you don't want to be with us for circle, you can go to the sand box or the book corner: those are the choices" [LF2.7]. And Max used to love to leave the room, simply run out. In gym one day, he tore out the gym door. Liz, busy giving hoops to children, said to me, "Did someone go out?" "Yes," I replied. She retrieved Max, telling him he cannot leave — she will think he is lost [LF2.6].

SUPPORTING PARENTS

One distinctive aspect of Liz's practical knowledge was her attitude toward the families of children in her care. She actively drew parents and siblings into her program, welcomed their participation, and showed an interest in the home life of her children. In fact, she built connections between the home life of the children and the life of the classroom, as the following examples illustrate.

Liz chatted easily with parents, who seemed to be around to a noticeable extent, and surprised me in our talks with what she knew about families of children in her care, including who was away in Vancouver, the names of their cats and dogs and which ones scratch: "We try to know them on a personal basis" [L6.4]. In the morning when parents arrive with children, she finds it a good time to "really talk to parents" [L1.4], both for context about the child but also to try to explain her program approach to them. In the fall, when she redeveloped the class schedule, she did up a version for parents to explain each segment and its purpose, using colloquial language accessible to them.

The parents of one child invited the class for snack and a visit at their home nearby. Liz took snapshots and wrote captions underneath, and these were displayed in the classroom and frequently mentioned on a visit I made soon afterward. On another occasion a parent was offered a book on fish to take home overnight because her child was suddenly so interested in them, cooking up crawfish in housekeeping, after a trip with his grandfather to taste lobster and crawfish at the fish market.

Sometimes when parents were drawn into her program the occasions were instances of both problem solving and of gift making. In circle, Liz invited Jane to bring her new green coat, handmade by her mother, to show the children how it looked with its new buttons.

> Yeah, her mom came in yesterday, and they were going to Woolco to buy buttons, and I said, "Well I have a big bucket of buttons here." . . . So we brought out this bucket of buttons, and she found one big white one. And then David found another one just like it. This was an enormous thing of buttons. So we found four buttons, and they were also exploring all the other buttons. . . . And her mother sewed them on last night and she wore it today, which was really interesting. And she was really pleased, her mom was really pleased. [L2.11]

In Liz's room there was a strong sense of connection to the families of children in her care. They were drawn into the life of the classroom, offered things that connected to their children's experience, made to feel welcome, and Liz's attitude toward them was consistently supportive.

In conclusion, Liz's teaching agenda was to provide positive experiences for her children, to encourage them to be active agents in control of their own play. The way she structured time and space, her corrections of children's actions, the genuine availability of materials in the classroom, the scripts for action that she used in interaction with the children — all had been constructed slowly (over more than a year) to support her teaching agenda. It was this coherence in her practical knowledge that I think gave a thrust or particular dynamic quality to her program: interesting things were always happening, and everyone, visitors included, could participate in them. To the outsider, the program felt like it was always opening out, with breathing space made for the things children and others thought of to do: even corrections did not feel so much like restrictions as like a chance to carve out a new path — and the child helped. The absence of patterns for teacher dominion was almost startling. The combination of circumstances that provoked this (broad experience as an early childhood educator, intensive in-service over time, temperament, and background) could lead one to wonder whether developmentally appropriate practice can be adequately constructed without such powerful elements in a teacher's work life. While this book cannot answer that, the next two chapters discuss some aspects of teacher practical knowledge that provide clues to this concern.

7 Developmental Appropriateness as a New Framework for Practice

The distinction between knowing-that and knowing-how has frequently been acknowledged and attributed to Ryle (Polanyi, 1958; Schön, 1983). As Polanyi describes, knowing how to do something involves tacit knowledge that is difficult to articulate, for much of it is subsumed as automatic. Riding a bicycle, playing the piano, and recognizing faces are examples of actions we may easily perform while being unable to describe how we do so. In terms of the ideology of developmentally appropriate practice, we can distinguish between knowing about this practice and having the performance skills to implement it. In addition to knowledge about something, and knowledge of how to do something, we can add our attitude toward it, its value to us, our motivation to do it. What I discovered is that a valuing of developmental appropriateness, according to teacher talk, does not necessarily coincide with high familiarity with this model of practice or with a high degree of implementation of it.

You have seen in the previous chapters that teacher-centered practice was a common feature of the day care settings observed and that implicit notions of preparation for school were important to these day care teachers. School life is the dominant presence in the life of children, outside the family, and the practice of these day care teachers frequently reflected this. Nor is it the case that aspects of developmentally appropriate practice were not recognized or utilized by these teachers, but that they did not have the overall impact upon practice expected by proponents of developmental appropriateness.

UNFAMILIARITY WITH ASPECTS
OF DEVELOPMENTALLY APPROPRIATE PRACTICE

There were six interrelated aspects of developmentally appropriate practice that were not fully utilized by four of the participants, whereas Liz was very comfortable with them. While some teachers, and Jill in particular, showed partial understanding and implementation of these aspects, others found some of them new and unfamiliar concepts of practice. The six aspects of developmentally appropriate practice that were somewhat unfamiliar were these:

1. Teacher observation of individual children as a basis for curriculum decisions
2. Teacher focus on child process in activity
3. An understanding of play and teacher roles to extend and support it
4. The importance of opportunities for child choices
5. The importance of child-initiated activity
6. Support for child problem solving

We will look at each of these unfamiliar aspects and see contrasting examples from practice that suggest familiarity and unfamiliarity. Then we will hear what teachers said about them. Examples from practice also display many other aspects of practice in addition to the one discussed, for much more is present in an example than can possibly be discussed in linear text.

Observation of Individual Children as a Basis for Curriculum Decisions

Observation as a basis for curriculum decisions requires a combination of knowledge about child development and alertness in the moment. Such observation involves attentiveness, watchfulness, and the ability to select from the stream of children's behavior the actions and talk that display individual children's interests, ideas, intentions, needs, and level of development. When Sebastian stuck the end of the skipping rope into a hole in the wall, Liz stopped Marcel from taking it out [FL1.8], saying, "He has a special idea for the string. . . . What's he going to do?" She selected Sebastian's action out of the stream of experience as an intention worthy of attention. The following vignettes show an instance of a teacher with this sort of watchfulness and an instance of a teacher whose agenda includes many things, but not close observation of children. We see the latter instance first.

> Sand play has been changed to a bin of Styrofoam pieces with scoops and measuring spoons. Sonia puts a music tape on, telling the substitute the record player keeps breaking. Two boys play in the Styrofoam. She goes over saying: "I didn't know we changed the sand play!"
>   Richard says, "Popcorn!"
>   Sonia replies, "When did we get that? Is it snow?"

Three girls rush over, hovering around the bin. Sonia leaves, taking a siphon of clear plastic with her. Three of the five children also leave; two more girls come, hanging back. Sonia is at the kitchen doing something with papers, talking to the substitute.

Five children play in the Styrofoam, making broad arm movements, chuffing and shuffling through it, scooping and pouring it out. Richard bites a piece, chews it. Girls take handfuls and walk to a shelf. Sonia approaches: "That's for inside the container. We can pretend it's snow. It's not like the other toys that we take to the table." She tells them the bits will get lost if they remove them from the bin.

Sonia leaves and enters a storage room, returning with blue construction paper and white chalk, arranging it on the craft table. She arranges chairs around another table, removes the sand play lid to the storage room.

The children say they are "making popcorn" in the Styrofoam.

Sonia sits at the craft table. "We can use chalk to make snow pictures. We can make anything we would do in the snow." [SF5.1,2]

Richard had an idea about the Styrofoam, an idea that was adopted by other children, but the teacher missed it, absorbed as she was with her own agenda, which included tidying up, organizing craft, and correcting. We know the consequences of Sonia's inattention to children's play, and we can see that if she does not notice it, she cannot support or extend children's language or representation, their personal scripts (Jones & Reynolds, 1992), or see that if she offers paper bags for the "popcorn," her correction to girls carrying it away may be unnecessary, and so forth.

In contrast, remember Liz observing and being alert to children's interest in the turtle when she had planned fingerpainting, or catching Bobby's interest in making "snow" when he spun cornstarch from the wheels of a toy car, or Nora observing the child painting her hand.

The point is not that teachers should always interrupt their own agenda to respond to what is emerging from the child—there has to be a balance of input from adults and children—but that she should observe it so that this information can be part of what she thinks about in deciding what to do.

Close observation of children's actions as a basis for curriculum decisions has, at the least, a century-long history. Montessori's work began with observation of children, rather than with design of a curriculum, and developed out of practical need (Montessori, 1964). Piaget, who was president of the Montessori Society in Switzerland in the 1920s (Kramer, 1976), spun his theories out of meticulous observation of child action

(Piaget, 1937/1954; 1945/1962). Observational studies of children expanded in the 1930s, and in laboratory preschools since the 1950s at least, observation has been a part of education for early childhood teachers (Read & Patterson, 1950/1980). Observation has always been closely linked with understanding children's development, with sensitivity to the differing world views of the child at particular points in her development (Hendrick, 1984; Hohmann et al., 1978; Lindberg & Swedlow, 1976).

Jill and Nora, in discussing observation, displayed a global sense of observing, "to see where the children are, to begin our programs and daily routines" [Jwc6]. Nora thought, she said, about what the group was most interested in talking about during a particular week: "work from there and do something that's fun that they want to do—they were talking about going out playing in the snow, so we did all our activities about snow" [N6.21]. Thus these two teachers used observation in a general way, directed toward the group as an entity rather than to individuals (although Jill also responded to individuals more in practice than her interview talk reflected).

Sonia and Carla both indicated that their concept of planning was circumscribed by weekly theme planning, finding general activities suitable for the group. Their awareness was of general characteristics and needs of the age group rather than a focus on individuals. Since Sonia did not attend to children's play, as shown in the example above, she missed much activity generated by the children, and Carla, though she did observe to assess use of materials, to add props or put them away, was highly attuned to her theme: "We have to follow that, we have to make theme, [each teacher] every 3 weeks" [C6.34]. Here we see her wanting to draw children's attention to aspects of her theme.

> Carla sits before an enormous bowl of red Jell-O, 11 children crowded around the table with her. She spoons it out into paper cups, saying, "Who can tell me what happened to the Jell-O?"
> "Look at the big hole!" says Bertram. She does not reply.
> "Remember Monday about touch? Feel and touch? Before you eat, I'll let you do something." She suggests they put one finger in to feel the Jell-O in their cup.
> "It's wibbly," says Angelica.
> "Is it soft or hard?" says Carla. "Is it hot or cold?" [CF5.1]

Her own agenda for vocabulary is so strong that she misses both Bertram's excitement at the excavated Jell-O and Angelica's precise description. Hers and the children's conversations do not meet in the middle, become mutual, although both have good things to offer.

Goffin (1989) reminds us of the importance of teacher planning:

> Descriptions of teacher planning document teachers' deliberate structuring of classroom content and organization. During planning, teachers formulate a course of action for carrying out instruction. Plans become scripts for carrying out teaching, and they change intentions into actions (pp. 191–192).

When planning is so focused on weekly themes, the teacher's agenda becomes narrowed to the chosen program content. Alertness to ideas and actions generated by children becomes difficult, for the teacher's mental space is absorbed by her attempts to convey her chosen content, to be a teacher in the conventional sense.

Focus on Children's Action Process

A focus on process reflects the emphasis in the ideology of developmentally appropriate practice on development of the whole child and the constructivist view of how the child learns (Duckworth, 1987; Forman & Hill, 1980; Kamii & DeVries, 1978/1993; Piaget, 1937/1954). Learning is neither segmented into subjects for mastery nor restricted to parts of the body, but involves the entire self, alert and concentrating. Since the young child learns concretely, in interaction with the social and material world, and only gradually over a period of years understands symbolic systems, then, logically, interaction with people and with physical material, as well as a focus on the child's actions in so doing, is the starting point for teacher action. The fact that the child is active and not passive, initiating and not simply receiving, generating rather than reproducing someone else's words and actions, reflects the value of the constructivist view of social and intellectual development.

When Sonia did her theme on shapes, she cut triangles, rectangles, squares, and circles out of sponges so children could make sponge prints of these shapes with paint as a craft activity. As she sat supervising the activity with those who chose to do this, she talked with them. Her talk focused primarily on colors or shapes, and guided the children to respond to her with "shape talk," thus focusing their attention on the theme; however, she made no mention of what their hands were doing with the sponges on the paper. Their actions were free to vary, but their wide, sweeping strokes or circling patterns went unremarked—their talk was constrained and separated from the processes in which their hands were engaged.

What shape are you using, Annie? Do you know what shape that is? That one's round.

Yes, I like your elephant. What shape did you use to make the elephant? [A square.] That isn't a square, that's a tri—[triangle]. Yes.

Eva, what shape's that? What shape are you using to make all that pretty blue [SV1]?

Her focus on theme talk—shapes in this case—shows both what is drawing her attention and what is absent from it. She does not remark on children's actions, on their processes in interacting with the materials. It was as if Sonia had imposed an aspect of developmentally appropriate practice—the belief that the process is more important than the product—on the content of a teacher-planned curriculum, but had not replaced the absence this leaves with the observation of process considered so important in developmentally appropriate practice.

In watching these teachers what struck me was that what was missing was the recognition that the *actions* of children express ideas, intentions, and incipient plans. While they were very focused on language, on talk and the importance of language development [the rationale behind every large-group activity! (N3.8; C4.7)], actions that the children made as they engaged with material were often overlooked.

Developmentally appropriate practice suggests that the focus of most activity for young children should be the child's interaction with material and people, with each child having his own materials and able to offer his own talk, rather than having talk and action constrained by group process, by teacher direction. This does not seem to be an easy thing to grasp, and Carla and I had an interesting discussion about this.

We don't discuss all the time [in circles]. We read stories or we sing songs . . . we bring the puppets in there . . . what did we do in group activities? Oh yes, they all cut the banana pieces and put them in the blender; they scoop the ice cream. They all had a turn to do that. Then I helped them to pour the milk and they drank it, what do you call it, milkshake. They do have opportunity to handle it. [C6.32]

Her insistence that children were active, after I had suggested that from what I saw, children mostly sat and listened and took turns with material as instructed in group activities, created an interesting tension for me. Here was a teacher who wanted to be seen as performing in developmentally appropriate ways and who honestly believed she did. My conception of the practice was different from hers, in that I did not see children in her setting as having *control* of the materials they were using. They were not able to make any decisions about what to do, and they were corrected quickly and efficiently if they did not follow her sequence of actions. Any activity outside the frame of doing as they were told at group times could quickly result in removal from the group. She thought they could sometimes do as they wanted but did not see the critical difference between having to wait to be told by the teacher that on this specific occasion their own actions with material were permitted and the alternative, where children know they can freely initiate interesting things to do. The fact that in six visits of 2 to 3 hours each I did not see occasions where children were permitted to interact freely with materials in group times also led me to think that such occasions were atypical. She clearly did not want to perceive these as atypical events: she saw them as a normal part of her practice.

Actions as a source of ideas upon which teachers could base their own response, a focus on child processes, was not widely present or understood by three of the participants. However, both Liz and Jill were sensitized to this and able to adjust group process to accommodate individual children, as shown by Jill's response to John's fingering of the pearl necklace.

Understanding and Supporting Children's Play

Accepting the ideas that children generate in play, and supporting their efforts to be makers, producers in the world (Gardner, 1978), suggests that teachers should understand their own role in play as one of positive intervention to extend and support children's interests and to encourage the development of more elaborated play. From a developmental point of view, the benefits of play are seen to be so profound for the child that active teacher support is necessary for good development (Bretherton, 1984; Bruner, Jolly, & Sylva, 1976; Christie & Johnson, 1983; Jones & Reynolds, 1992; Smilansky, 1968; Sutton-Smith, 1969).

Liz actively intervened in play to extend it, to model possibilities for her young 2-year olds, to demonstrate possibilities in using material, to open up a world of action and thought for them. When Bobby spun cornstarch off the wheel of a dinky to make snow, she saw his excitement and provided a water wheel to spin in the sand box. Ambrose pretended to cook fish in housekeeping, which led to a wider interest in fish and a donation of lobsters by a parent. The lobsters swam in the water play tub until they were cooked for lunch, an event of great interest to the children.

Somebody was talking about pollywogs, and we brought them in, we got them in the classroom, got books on them, so we've extended on that. All day long we extend on their play. Oh, gosh, we're doing a good job! Just now when I think about the whole thing. [L6.24]

With interventions, of course if there's a problem or something they can't do, I would intervene right away. If things are going really nicely, you know, I like to be in there too. . . . Interventions can sometimes be very quick. You walk by, or you give
Yeah, a look?
Yeah, "I see what you're doing," and keep going. Housekeeping keeps coming to mind, because I'm intervening in there a lot. We're doing a lot of dramatic play, and I'm the baby. I'm mostly baby. [L6.25]

Liz followed this with a description of what she does when she plays baby — crying and throwing away her bottle — and how astonished the children are and how they try to help "the baby." She actively played with children in housekeeping, taking on a role in the play so that children could react to her in the role. Besides the fact that such play was fun, she was aware of using it to extend children's language and role understanding: "the language again, that's me with the language, going in" [L6.25].

For the other teachers, the notion of extending children's play was somewhat foreign. Jill saw the idea of extension as referring to giving children more *time* to play; but she also recognized that her routine truncated play, made its continuation more difficult [J6wc2]. Certainly an inhibitor of play is a tightly structured routine in which play is restricted by the clock. Sonia, Nora, and Carla thought they themselves were not needed in children's play, so that their intervention was primarily to correct. Sonia, for example, missed out on Richard's transformation of the Styrofoam into popcorn and corrected the girls who began moving it around, without knowledge of the children's intention or consideration of the possibility that it could legitimately have been extended. To support play the teacher interprets the intentions of children and permits them space, rather than simply correcting activity that does not fit her agenda.

Whether play is accepted or not is causally connected to the corrections of the teacher: if playful actions do not fit her mental set for what should be happening, then she will inhibit those actions. Clearly the practice of closing off areas of play from children's use, a frequent practice in Sonia's, Nora's, and Carla's settings, is at odds with both developmentally appropriate notions of play and the teacher's role in supporting and encouraging it. Since these teachers also frequently corrected children in play, either by removing material or children from play, the cumulative effect of these two practices was to reduce and truncate the opportunities for play in their settings.

A lack of understanding of the positive role of the teacher in encouraging the development and elaboration of play in developmentally appropriate practice may have made it more difficult to see the impact of their practices regarding access to resources. Yet their positive valuing of play suggests that this effect was unintended. Carla displayed this clear valuing of support for play.

Initially Carla did not understand the language in which I tried to express this understanding of the teacher's role as one who extends and supports play. "What is it? Can you explain it?" [C6.32] she asked, but then, once it was explained, she spoke passionately in its favor. "I think it's *most* important, I do think it is important. I think it's a good idea to extend it" [C6.33]. In her setting, children played mostly on their own, except when corrected, but she felt this was due to constraints, pressure to monitor a large group.

> You really don't [have time], like when two people [staff] are gone from the room and you really actually don't have time to sit down and play with them.
> *Would you prefer to?*
> Yes. In the morning I do. I like to sit with them. . . . This is the main thing in preschool or day care, you are one of them. You're the friend. You like to share things with them, although they have other friends. You are not like a teacher or boss telling them what to do all the time. . . . Actually you are there to play with them. [C6.33–34]

Nora, by the time of our final interview, was pleased that she was intervening less to correct than previously; this was part of an experience of major change that she underwent over the course of the year. As yet, however, she had little sense of positive interventions.

> Orlando and Raphael were playing in the water, and they were pretending there was a storm. It was [all] over the floor, and you know, I just accepted it like it was, and after they were finished, they dried their hands, I just got them the mop. And they were having a great storm! Yeah, well, it was green water and just the way they were talking, the clouds are here, and it's raining and it's storming, look at the waves, how big they are. [N6.17]

She said that earlier in the year she would have "jumped in" to correct them for spilling water on the floor. At this point, she saw herself as able to tolerate the consequences of their play without interrupting it to correct or stop it when she believed such an intervention was unnecessary. The way she spoke conveyed her pleasure in this newfound practice.

Overall, my sense of their understanding was that for four teachers, the idea of positive interventions in and extension of play was unfamiliar and their concepts of these underdeveloped, but whatever sense they made of the idea, it was something they valued.

The Importance of Providing Choices

A choice allows a child to make a decision about what to do. It keeps the child engaged in the world, with some sense of having an impact upon it. As well, a choice is a free move and gives the child a tiny bit of power. A choice is also a plan, an intention to do. Control of one's own agenda, a chance to direct the actions one takes, is seen as central both to developmental appropriateness and human learning (Dreikurs, 1964; Hendrick, 1984; Hohmann et al., 1978; Rogers, 1969).

The concept of child choice and decision making is a highly prioritized value in models of developmental appropriateness. Where each teacher provided for some child choice, particularly in the context of free play, they differed in the extent to which they extended child decision making across the other contexts of their programs.

Only Liz saw it as applying to all facets of the children's day, consciously building choice into all group times and into common routines such as bathroom and snack: "That's the point in this classroom is choices. You know you can make the choice" [L2.17]. As discussed earlier, even her corrections would offer choice to a child to help him move back into activity, as in, "You need to choose another bike; which one are you going to choose?" [LF1.7]. As well, children in her program were not obligated to attend large-group circles: there were always one or two other choices available to them. While most children would be with Liz at the rug, a child might be playing in the sand box or looking at books.

However, choice as a valued aspect of practice was not well understood by several of the teachers.

Carla invites each child individually by name to retrieve the show-and-tell item from a carton where they are stored. This takes several minutes. I wonder why the box isn't brought to the table? With all the items on the table, she then has them guess from her verbal description which one she has chosen — a small airplane. The owner picks it up and holds it, while the other children are asked, in order of their seating arrangement, to ask a question of the owner.

"Now, Gary, you can start asking him a question. No, you guys have to listen."

"I don't know what to ask."

This takes a very long time, as there are eight children and they have difficulty thinking of questions.

"Where did you get it? When did you get it?" are asked over and over. There are one or two genuine questions. "Can it fly high?"

It starts again for the next item, all the way around through eight questions or nonquestions, and continues through nine items. By this time, the children have sat for 40 minutes, their only activity holding an object for a few minutes and trying to think of eight questions. They waited, they wiggled, they tried to be attentive, but it became increasingly difficult. Because story and snack preceded this, with the exception of a few minutes going to the bathroom, the children had been sitting for an hour, this upon arrival from school. [FC4.2–3]

"That was for language development" [C4.7], Carla said, and "the main thing in day care or preschool, some children or maybe [the] majority, [their] attention span is not that good, they are so young" [C4.9]. She wanted each child to ask a question about every child's proffered toy, a sort of Socratic method in reverse, and her focus was stretching attention span, listening skills, and language. The concept of child choice is clearly absent from such teacher-centered frameworks for action. As well, choice may be seen to be incompatible with a prioritizing of listening skills and attention span.

One question is whether such absences are a deliberate decision or a lack of familiarity with developmentally appropriate values and how to implement them. Because of the cumulative impact of Carla's statements valuing developmentally appropriate practice, both in interviews and in discussing the criteria, I think it was lack of familiarity.

Interestingly, four of the five teachers did not realize that our discussion of choice applied to all contexts within day care. They said yes, the children could choose material, choose what to do, but they did not realize that the concept of choice in developmentally appropriate practice applies to every time frame: they applied it to free play and not to teacher-centered group times [S7.11; J6.8; N6.14]. I infer that they assumed the criteria could not refer to group times, since child choice and control of material are not conventionally a major part of teacher-centered instruction. They removed from consideration all the things they do—crafts,

group circles—that reflect another framework for action, teacher dominion. The fact that four teachers omitted reference to group activities and
to time organization in considering opportunities for choice is further argument that their allegiance to frameworks for action is split between two
contradictory models.

They were much more comfortable considering choice with reference
specifically to free play. Jill supported children fully in play, but this
context was very distinct from other time segments in her setting. But even
during play, Sonia, Carla, and Nora had patterns of closing off entire
areas and rendering them inaccessible during play. All three of these
teachers would prefer, so they said, to keep areas open, offering more
choices to children. Sonia and Carla blamed constraints—time pressures,
lack of space, and pressure to monitor while insufficiently staffed—for
closing off areas during play. This bothered Sonia: "it's an awful thing to
have all these centers closed . . . and they'd do so much better if they were
allowed to go in all those areas" [S7.10]. Carla took it in stride: "it doesn't
bother me that much, because it's open again, you know" [C6.22–23].
Although in theory she "would like to open it all the time," she does not
see this as possible [C6.22].

Although I have every confidence that the four teachers thought they
understood the concept of child choice and thought they met it, their
notion of this was bounded by the sole context of free play. They assumed
it applied merely to free play and did not address the totality of time and
space in their setting as a single context. This suggests that their practice is
deeply split into two compartments or conflicting spheres held in tandem
as separate frameworks for conducting practice in day care.

The Importance of Child-Initiated Activity

Child-initiated activity is purposeful activity, deciding to do something
and carrying it out, with teacher support. It is opportunity to initiate
actions, activity, ideas, and plans and take responsibility for completing
them (Schweinhart, 1988). It is a broader category of activity than play,
for it includes activities such as looking at books, writing stories, experi-
menting with bubbles, making discoveries about how the world works—
activities that are not imaginative but attempt to address the real world.
Liz's understanding and support of Tina's desire to see the umbrella
opened and feel what it was like to stand underneath it was one instance
when child-initiated activity was welcomed. Another was her dropping of
her plan to fingerpaint when the children wanted to watch and talk about
the turtle, relating it to their television experience.

The notion of child-initiated activity was new to several teachers. For

Sonia, it was so new that she was unable to respond, except to say that she thought she was "too rigid" in welcoming children's ideas, that she wanted to be more spontaneous in including them in her program [S7.13–14]. Carla did not recognize the term and asked: "What's that? Can you explain that?" [C6.28]. When it was explained, she described instances when she took children's ideas and developed them into program, in one case a theme on jewelry making and in another, on tools and machines. Her way of extending children's ideas was to turn them into contexts for teacher instruction. Both Nora and Carla saw child-initiated activity simply as child selection of material in free play: "that they should go to the shelf and take out the crayons and paper sort of thing" [N6.18], as Nora put it. Although this is part of the concept, it is a narrower conception than intended by the ideology of developmental appropriateness. Here is an example of how possibilities for child-initiated activity were unwittingly deflected.

> "We're going to make pumpkin masks today." Carla passes out orange paper and gives instructions to nine children at her table.
> "I'm making a rooster!" says a boy.
> "We're making pumpkins. You can make a rooster another day."
> "I'm going to make a snowman," says another. She either does not hear this or chooses not to respond. After an interruption from children wanting the housekeeping area open, she says, "Make a nice pumpkin." . . .
> The finished masks vary in shape, placement of eyes and mouth, etcetera. They all made pumpkins — no roosters or snowmen. [CF1.9,11]

Carla explained her response to me:

> Now in this one, that was the Halloween theme, we have to decorate the room. So they were told they have to make the Halloween symbols. So pumpkin is one of the symbols, so that's why I asked them to make the pumpkin. It was going with the theme. [C6.12]

Carla had a strong belief in taking responsibility to ensure interesting activity for the children — adding rocks to paint when she thought string painting might not be sufficient to interest them, adding containers to water play when a child in an arm cast could not use what was there [C3.13–14]. She articulated what she actively thought about in preparing such activities, "the ability, age, and my ideas" [C2.17], saying they have to match the children's interest. What was absent was a sense of letting ideas emerge from the children. When she asked me what child-initiated activity was, it suggested that this was simply something she did not know about.

The Importance of Problem Solving

The ability to generate solutions, to think up different things to do when facing a problem, and the ability to anticipate consequences are considered fundamental to healthy adjustment (Shure & Spivak, 1978). These abilities prevent frustration and build competence. Taking the initiative is the opposite of passivity; trying to solve a problem is the opposite of helplessness. The rationale in developmentally appropriate practice is that problem solving builds confidence, competence, and a sense of ability in handling the world: ability to handle small problems is sound preparation for handling larger ones, as well as making life more comfortable for the moment. The concept of "scaffolding" is also useful here (Bruner, 1986; Vygotsky, 1978), for it describes how adults surround children with talk that helps children to do more than they are capable of on their own. Such talk conveys to children a range of possibilities for thinking.

Liz understood problem solving and made use of it constantly in her work [and was the one teacher who labeled her practice as developmentally appropriate (L6.15)]. Here is her response when I asked what problem solving would look like in her setting:

> "What could we do about that?" If they're having a problem with another child . . . or they need something to stick with this, "Well what could we do about that? Looks like you need something more." I mean, if they just can't even see that, I'll say, "Well, there are some things over here, let's go over."
>
> I try to keep it open. Depending on the child, some children will say, "Well, I need glue." "Where do we find the glue?" Some children may not even know they need glue or tape, so depending on the child, of course.
>
> We go through the steps of what — "And I can see that you're really angry, and that's okay. And I know you really want that truck, but you can't have it right now. What can we do about that? Is there another truck? Where can we find a truck?"
>
> "How did that make you feel?" You know, these kind of things. "What could you say to him instead of 'No'"? "I don't like it when you take my car" or "it makes me sad when you broke my playdough." [L6.21]

Other examples of how other teachers handled similar types of situations follow.

> At the sandbox, Charles and Gordon struggle to hold the same rubber dinosaur. Sonia, arriving, says: "Charles, did Gordon have it in his hand?"
> "Me have it my hand, too," says Charles.
> "Who had it in their hand first?" asks Sonia.
> Charles flashes his hand up in the air like a schoolchild with the right answer. Gordon looks insistent, perplexed, says he had it. Sonia takes the dinosaur in her hand. "Someone's not telling the truth. Only one person can have it in their hand." More conversation, too low for the mike to pick up. The boys' heads hang and Sonia leaves, taking the dinosaur with her. [FS4.18]

As we watched this incident on the video, Sonia said to me: "I didn't know what to do with these two. I didn't know. Usually I can tell, but I couldn't tell—I couldn't get them to admit to me which one had it" [S4.17]. Sonia's usual concern in such a conflict was that children share materials by turn-taking. Her more typical reaction, she thought, would be to say, "Well, why don't you play with it for a little while, and then let him play with it for a little while" [S7.3]. Turn-taking focuses the child's attention on social interchange, halts one child's play at a time, but leaves the dinosaur in circulation as a play object. On this occasion Sonia removed the dinosaur, leaving both boys displaying body posture that I read as disappointment. They left the sandbox shortly afterwards.

Apart from Liz, the criteria representing problem-solving techniques were difficult for the teachers to discuss and required considerable explanations on my part. I felt they were "grasping at straws" to try to understand problem-solving techniques. At the same time, it was clear that they liked the idea of problem solving and would like it to be part of their practice. The following examples attempt to show both the appeal and the strangeness of problem solving to them.

Carla referred to problem solving as situations in which a child complained to her about, for example, being hit, and she would say, "Why don't you talk to them, [tell them] you don't like to be hit by somebody" [C6.26]. Humans take actions such as hitting when they have run out of other resources to try, and problem solving with children is an attempt to build up those other resources. Problem solving is such that, if it were actively undertaken, the children would find more solutions without hurting other children. I could accept that Carla thought she problem solved with children, but not that her concept and that intended by the ideology referred to the same thing.

Nora and Jill clearly valued problem solving and were conscious of trying to assist it, but they saw it as a situation in which teachers would direct children toward a solution rather than helping children to generate solutions of their own.

I'm going to help them, but I'm not going to do it for them; I'm going to show them how to do it. [J6.10]

Sometimes the solution is easier to tell them than to let them solve it. [N6.16]

Sonia was quite unfamiliar with the notion of problem solving as it applied to her practice. "Problem solving? I don't know. As in? . . . I'm not sure. Problem solving as in?" [S7.12]. As she asked me for examples, I felt she was actively seeking what she did not yet know and was prepared to absorb any idea that added to her sense of it.

The most intriguing aspect in asking teachers about problem solving was the reaction of the three whose understanding was partial. Sonia, Jill, and Nora all actively sought what these criteria might mean. Here are examples of Jill's and Sonia's reactions to my explanations, in which I used the example of two children fighting over a plastic dinosaur:

If they were fighting over a dinosaur — there wasn't enough — I'd probably say, "You have to wait till they're finished." Yeah, that's what I would do. Or try to find another one. But I probably wouldn't suggest something else for a dinosaur. I will now. [J6.10]

No, no I don't find I do that. I think actually it's a great way to do things, but I don't think it's something I do. [S7.12–13]

We try to redirect them when they come to us with it [a problem], but not in the other sense of actually saying okay, this is you guys having a problem, and maybe we could find a solution by thinking about what you could do to make things better, how could you both win sort of situation. [S7.12,12]

I felt these two teachers in particular left the interview with a different sense of problem solving than when we started. Most obvious was the felt reaction that all five placed a high value on problem solving as an idea.

Even the teacher who had the least notion of it wanted to be seen as performing it.

A predisposition to accept aspects of developmentally appropriate practice as having something valuable to offer, while being somewhat unsure of certain important aspects, suggests a tension between teachers' current practical knowledge and some glimpse of desirable possibilities just beyond. Liz understood and struggled to implement these aspects of developmentally appropriate practice. The others obviously wanted to be seen to do so and were able to suggest ways in which they *did* carry out parts of it.

DIFFICULTIES IN CONSTRUCTING DESIRED PRACTICE

Greene (1988) notes that each of us has "horizons of understanding," that there are boundaries, edges beyond which we cannot see. It is difficult to be aware of what we do not know. Once awareness is roused, action is possible. If teachers have never been exposed to something, how can they be expected to know it, let alone implement it in practice? This chapter has dealt with areas of developmentally appropriate practice that were unfamiliar to several of the five participants. The lack of familiarity with these integral aspects of developmentally appropriate practice is not unusual, for they are aspects that are new in the theory of early childhood, having been widely developed only in the past 20 years. However, although these may be sophisticated aspects of practice, the model does not work without them. They are essential. I was led to consider why these aspects in particular might be so unfamiliar.

Whether there has been adequate exposure to them in training is an obvious question but beyond the scope of this exploration of teachers' practical knowledge. As well, there may have been inadequate exposure to them in practicum settings, because they are so new. Nevertheless, even with adequate training and practicum experience, these aspects may not be sufficiently understood or absorbed, and there is a particular reason why this might be so. It concerns the language that describes the model.

The model of developmentally appropriate practice contains some terminology that is specific to description of concepts of the model, words that must be addressed as new vocabulary by one learning the model. Phrases or terms such as *interventions* or *extensions in children's play*, *child-initiated activity*, and *child-centered program* are not part of the common vocabulary of teachers and require interpretation in light of the model. If a teacher is unfamiliar with these concepts, exposing her to the ideas, the "knowing-that" aspect, is relatively straightforward. A teacher, such as Sonia or Carla, who discovers a new concept, such as child-initiated activity, can do something about finding out about it: it is no longer beyond the horizon of her vision. Any performance skill requires an apprenticeship, and if the ideas appeal to her, she can begin the arduous process of attempting to construct these in her practice.

There is a second problem with the language through which the ideology is expressed. Much of the language that is used to describe the model of developmentally appropriate practice is the language of everyday use — words and phrases such as *observation*, *a focus on process*, and *active learning*. I submit that one problem with conveying the model to teachers is that the words have one meaning, congruent with the model, to the teacher educator, but that student teachers may assimilate such familiar terms to present intellectual structures, rather than grasping that the concept behind the terms is different from their normal understanding of the word.

Both teacher dominion and developmental appropriateness, for example, emphasize language development, but in teacher-centered practice the emphasis is on teacher instruction and the goal of fluency in reading. In developmental appropriateness, with the stress on active learning, the emphasis is on *action* first (child action) supplemented by language which connects to that action and so has meaning for the child (Hendrick, 1984; Hohmann et al., 1978). The reader will recall that several of my participants used language in isolation, for example, in crafts connected to theme content, entirely ignoring the child's process in acting upon material. Four of the five participants, in fact, paid little attention to children's actions. Interestingly, language development was the major rationale for most group activities, a context in which possibilities for action were generally suspended. Teachers had absorbed a belief in the efficacy of language for intellectual development but stressed this in teacher-centered rather than developmentally appropriate ways. In April I noted in my journal:

> I am slowly becoming convinced that teachers do not think much about children's actions, for example, with their hands, and how they connect to thought. Remember Sonia's sponge-painting craft, where she talked about shapes and ignored movement of hands entirely. Child process went unremarked. And Jill's wishing they would do her idea in craft, faces "the way they should be," rather than their own idea, and the focus on talk alone at circle among Jill, Sonia, and Carla. The idea that when hands do something — successfully construct a bridge with blocks or a face with a crayon — that something has been learned, an internal mental structure effected, seems very foreign to teachers yet is at the heart of notions of child development.

A second example of this difficulty with the everyday language of the model is the term *observation*. Teachers hear of its importance and assume that because they monitor children, they are observing. But there is a vast difference between observing solely for safety problems and observing to note intentions behind children's actions and act upon them, such as Liz's response to Gary's desire in play to have "milk" from Dryden's milk carton. Teachers cannot observe something they do not know: again, it is beyond that metaphorical horizon of vision, and without an adequate understanding of the theoretical framework, the developmental expectations for children in the preschool years, they will bring previously formed notions of concepts for such words as *observation* to bear on their learning of the model. Conveying the nuances of a different meaning for common words may be problematic for teacher educators.

One can hypothesize that understanding developmentally appropriate practice requires a shift in mental framework, an accumulation of specific understandings until some threshold is reached beyond which nothing is ever quite the same again. One of Greene's metaphorical horizons has been crossed. Or, to use the Piagetian metaphor (Nelson, 1977), one no longer assimilates material to present structures but shifts or accommodates the structures, in the process acquiring new possibilities for action.

It may be the case that developmentally appropriate practice is neither easily nor simply grasped. Sonia's reaction in reading her feedback paper was, as you remember, traumatic, because she valued the idea of beginning with the child but saw, in contrast, how her highly programmatic approach covered up much of what might emerge from the children. Each of the five participants was different in the extent to which she understood and implemented these six unfamiliar aspects of developmentally appropriate practice. What was impressive was that all, no matter the degree of understanding or implementation, strongly valued the ideology and preferred to be seen as adopting it where possible. Although it is possible to attribute some of this to my presence as a researcher, it is also instructive, for it suggests a willingness, a motivation to make a commitment to carry out developmentally appropriate practice.

If teachers were familiar with these aspects of the model of developmental appropriateness, they could themselves make a decision as to whether this was practice that they wished to attempt to implement. However, they could not consciously implement these practices if they were unknown. In fact, there were several instances in which teachers implemented in practice something they could not name or did not recognize in talking about it. Think of Jill responding to Jason's hand flexing over the bead necklace in show and tell, responding to his action as idea, yet telling me once she didn't see the children as having many ideas [J6.11], or Sonia's saying she wished she were more spontaneous and yet agreeing to join the research project after a mere 10 minutes of discussion.

These teachers had the courage to share their practical knowledge with me, aware that I was interested in how it fit the ideology. However, what our final interview showed me above all else was the pain of wanting to be constructing valued practice and not fully grasping what is meant by that. If these teachers could implement appropriate practice to the extent they were, based on partial knowledge, think what they could be doing, and the confidence and reassurance it would provide, if they were fully comfortable with the model.

The teachers who best understood the criteria characterizing developmentally appropriate practice (Liz and Jill) also selected this as a model of practice like their own. Where the model was familiar, known, it was implemented. Where the model was less understood, it was also less implemented. One the one hand, this is just as we expect; on the other, all participants valued developmentally appropriate practice and wanted to implement it. The question then becomes, if the motivation is present, the eagerness to make a commitment, why the difference in familiarity with and grasp of the model? All the teachers had received extensive training in the past 10 years. It was interesting that the three who best understood the model had all received their training in the same program. Clearly one area of interest to teacher educators is the specific effects of training, and this result raises the question whether the other programs adequately convey developmentally appropriate practice. Alternatively, perhaps it has more to do with the stance of the day care center itself, the "overarching theory" appropriated by the center as its own, what it communicates to staff as desired practice.

Other researchers have noted some of the same phenomena as emerged in this study. Snider (1990, p. 75) found, in a study relating teacher education and work experience to knowledge of developmentally appropriate practice, that teachers' knowledge of developmentally appropriate practice was low if they had not been trained specifically in five areas:

1. Observing and recording children's behavior
2. Creating learning environments
3. Creating, evaluating, and selecting materials
4. Curriculum models
5. The planning, implementation, and evaluation of developmentally appropriate content

The findings in the present study suggest that teachers are unfamiliar with several important aspects of developmentally appropriate practice, and these overlap with Snider's findings. In particular, if teachers do not observe children closely, other aspects of developmentally appropriate practice cannot follow.

I noted earlier Goffin's (1989) observation that teaching lacks a history of practice. Paley's (1985, 1990) documentation of teaching kindergarten and Lillard's (1980) on a Montessori classroom are prototypes for such collections of practical knowledge and its evolution. What this suggests is that we need to write about teachers' struggles to construct developmentally appropriate practice to help make it familiar, to bring it into the open as something to be discussed, debated, and reflected upon.

8 | Scripts and Reflection in Teacher Practical Knowledge

Teachers both inherit scripts for action that they continue to use day by day and make plans in ways that perpetuate previously scripted routines for program. But as well, they also change these scripts in both minute and major ways, as they generate new responses to problems in their work. These problem-solving attempts may be termed reflection-in/on-action. Here we will examine some examples of scripts for action and of reflection-in/on-action. At what point does reflection break the automaticity of previously scripted patterns? I will argue that both the location and the extent of reflection-in/on-action is different in teacher dominion and developmentally appropriate practice.

A major difficulty for teachers who value and hope to construct developmentally appropriate practice is the fact that they may be perpetuating scripts for teacher dominion long in place in settings and unreflectively think that these are adequate to developmental appropriateness, when in fact they undercut it. It is difficult to reflect on these taken-for-granted patterns. In particular, it is the scripts concerning organization of time that seem most difficult to surface and reconstruct. Several of the teachers whose work you have seen inherited scripts for action that became tacit, taken-for-granted patterns of functioning. These inherited scripts may be developmentally appropriate or teacher-centered, but I found that whatever was currently in place tended to be adopted as validated practice; this chapter will, in part, illustrate this. Because the teacher-centered scripts were closed-ended, teacher-controlled, tacitly understood, and performed at speed, they undercut reflection. But teachers do also manage to change their practice, and we will review some examples of reflection as they occurred among these teachers. What emerged was a difference in the scope and quality of reflection between those following teacher-centered versus more developmentally appropriate practice.

Schank and Abelson (1977) argue that a script "is a structure that describes appropriate sequences of events in a particular context"; it is a "predetermined, stereotyped sequence of actions that defines a well-known situation" (p. 41). A script is, in part, a plan to achieve a goal (Mandler, 1984). Institutions in particular are subject to stereotyped scripts as routine roles are carried out. In any endeavor that requires repeated performance, such as day care teaching, scripts for routine events are quickly formed and become automatic: this is because simpler skills are gradually subsumed into larger wholes, as in the example Polanyi (1958) uses, where the skill necessary in using a hammer becomes subordinated in consciousness to a focus on the task of hitting the head of the nail. The subordinated skills are taken for granted. Taking some things for granted, attention can be focused on key matters.

What should also be clear from the outset is that any form of practice has typical scripts for action that can easily become tacit practice for teachers. These occur wherever actions or interactions are repeated frequently. Whether a day care teacher follows teacher dominion or developmental appropriateness, or some other framework for action, she constructs or adopts scripts for routine actions as the bedrock of her practice. And simply because they are enacted, there is a tendency to insist that they are necessary, even if this contradicts other values, as we saw in Sonia's and Carla's situations. But I argue that the scripts in developmentally appropriate practice are of a different character — more open-ended and flexible — than in teacher dominion, as the following brief examples show. Liz said that she gave children a running commentary on their actions, that this was terribly important for their language development, and that she did this running commentary automatically: "I just do it now, I don't even realize [I'm doing it]" [L2.9]. She performed this kind of descriptive talk so continuously and repeatedly for children that it was clear that doing so had become an automatic script for action. Another example is Nora's newly acquired script for observing a child's actions, rather than jumping in with immediate correction; think of her permitting the child to paint the skin of her own hand. A third example is the class of sentences that Liz [L6.21] used to begin a problem-solving situation: "What could we do about that?" or "Where can we find another _____ ?"

Before examining reflection in these teachers' work, I want to look briefly at how teacher-centered scripts were tacitly accepted as necessary in their practice.

SCRIPTS FOR TEACHER DOMINION

Among the teachers with whom I worked, scripts for much teacher-centered activity in day care were in place in settings, quickly adopted by teachers and perpetuated without reflection. This is not a criticism of teachers: it is the nature of repetitive work to be done automatically. However, in settings where teacher-centered practice predominates, the fact that this becomes automatic practice so quickly and easily through repetition of lived experience makes developmentally appropriate practice more difficult to construct.

Eisner (1985) points out that

> schools prepare most people for positions and contexts that in many respects are quite similar to what they experienced in school as students: hierarchical organization, one-way communication, routine; in short, compliance to purposes set by another. (p. 91)

Where the teacher steps into this set of scripts in day care, the implicit expectation is that now it is her turn to set the purposes, to prepare the agenda for action. Grant and Sleeter (1985), in a 3-year study of a mid-western American school, noted the tendency for teachers to perpetuate traditional teaching practice, suggesting a failure of imagination on the teachers' part to produce innovative practice. Hatton (1987) countered their argument with the suggestion that practice is circumscribed more by context (use of time, in particular) than they recognized, as well as by teacher images of practice, of the teacher as arbiter of social control.

The notion that teachers' mindsets, or conceptions of knowledge, are derived from teachers' work situations and experience—that is, from practical contexts rather than theory or training—is frequently acknowledged (Connelly & Clandinin, 1986; Nias, 1986; Sachs, 1987). Meaning is derived from lived experience, and the script for action provides predictability for the actor; it reduces uncertainty.

How do scripts for teacher dominion become a part of a particular teacher's repertoire? Two powerful routes to the adoption of scripts were evident in working with these teachers. First, scripts for teacher-centered activity were *inherited* by teachers as patterns that define day care work. Second, teacher *planning* of theme content was closely connected to the construction of scripts for teacher dominion. With a fixed schedule marking a time for circle, craft, and play, personal patterns quickly became entrenched. Inheriting scripts from others and constructing scripts out of teacher plans were two routes to acquiring scripts for teacher-centered practice in day care. Each type can be called up and enacted when triggered by action rules (Halkes, 1988) that connect teacher theory with presently lived experience.

Scripts as Inherited Routines

When an early childhood teacher begins work in the setting, unless the center is brand-new, she inherits a package of routine uses for time and space. For the day care teacher, patterns of handling groups of children, of organizing the day into time frames, of moving the children through space and time are passed on to her in the midst of their enactment in the present, with the implicit expectation that she will continue them. It is necessary for the functioning of the institution.

Jill demonstrated this impact of inherited patterns on her practice. For instance, she has always used themes and has never questioned this: it is part of her history. Perhaps you recall her saying, "That was the way it was when I came and I guess I think that's the way it should be done, so that's the way I do it" [J1.17–18]. I had asked her what provides the structure for her program: I knew she knew this intimately, because she successfully performed it daily. However, she could not articulate it for me, because it was, as Polanyi would say, implicit or tacit knowledge.

> I just follow the footsteps.
> *What footsteps?*
> Well the day care, that's the way they do it. They have circle
> and they have craft, and I mean I've changed a few things. But
> that's, when I started, that's the way the person I worked with did it,
> and I just keep doing it. All these years. [J2.5]

Here we see the power of the scripts in place in the setting to suggest their own continuation. They are followed because they are in place: lived practice has the force of expected practice.

Liz, too, said that she had used teacher-centered practice for 7 years, until the intervention of the High/Scope in-service. If nothing else, such statements demonstrate the critical importance of the initial patterns or scripts for action undertaken in a setting: they have the power to prescribe the future, simply because they are in place.

Scripts in place in a setting, whether teacher-centered or developmentally appropriate, can become part of a teacher's practice without conscious reflection or judgment on the part of either teacher or administration. In Nora's case, for instance, it became clear in our final interview that the practice of closing play areas because of misuse (such as closing housekeeping when it was not adequately tidied) was a pattern inherited by Nora's colleague. Neither teacher was comfortable with it; but both had followed a practice neither liked, for months in one case and years in the other.

However, inherited ways of handling transitions and adhering to time frames for program content were not the only events around which teachers adopted scripts for action in day care.

Scripts as Teacher Plans

Goffin (1989), who also cites Shavelson on this point, notes that plans become scripts. "During planning, teachers formulate a course of action for carrying out instruction. Plans become scripts for carrying out teaching, and they change intentions into actions" (pp. 191–192). Teachers can plan in a style that supports either developmental appropriateness or teacher dominion. Developmentally appropriate planning leaves space for child agency and is more open-ended; teacher-centered plans tend to be more tightly scripted to meet specific teacher objectives, regardless of children's intentions. In the work of four of these teachers, there was a problematic aspect of planning that resulted in teacher-centered scripts.

Theme planning, as it was done by Sonia, Carla, and Jill, was basically the construction of scripts for teacher dominion into which children's responses would fit in prescribed ways. Sonia's shape circle and Carla's smelling jar circle demonstrate this. As well, scripts for action are present in every song and fingerplay that a teacher selects, in crafts in which the teacher plans a specific product and how it is to be accomplished, in dittos and coloring book pages that announce to the child a program for coloring. Games in music, board and card games — they all announce a particular script, a prescribed sequence of actions, or rules, that follow from selection of the script. When the teacher chooses any of these as part of her planned activities, she is choosing specific scripts that she already knows [or memorizes or reminds herself of with notes close by (JF1.10; SF5.3)]. The action plan is set, and the activity consists in carrying out the prescribed sequence to accomplish the event. In experiencing these, the child lives out a given script with prescribed social content. In fact, these games, crafts, songs, stories, fingerplays, and theme content that form the bulk of a day care teacher's curriculum in some settings are scripted vehicles for the transmission of social knowledge.

The Intersection of Teacher-Centered Script and Child-Initiated Activity

These scripts for transmitting social knowledge in teacher-centered activities are a one-way communication. The difficulty with such scripts for action, from the perspective of developmentally appropriate practice, is that they omit the possibility of child participation in controlling or directing the agenda for action. Where, in such scripted events, is there room for the child's idea, the child's song, the child's invention or discovery about the world? Where is there even any expectation that such might be forthcoming from the child? If the teacher has filled all the time with previously constructed scripts, what chance to participate in the construction of her own knowledge does the child retain? Yet from the perspective of developmentally appropriate practice, this is precisely how the child learns — by attempting to make sense of her own experiences with materials and people, not someone else's experience, not rote rules or action patterns (Duckworth, 1987).

A situation that occurred with Sonia illustrates this point. During the musical shapes game, Sebastian wanted to rejoin the children crawling around the remaining paper shapes on the floor. He was returned to his shape on the sidelines, because he was "out." At the end of the game, he was upset and crying, and Sonia held him on her lap on the floor. As we watched this on video, she reported what he was saying: "Something about being an elephant, he wants to be an elephant, he wants to crawl around" [S3.13]. On the video, we hear Sonia suggest "sleeping elephants," and she tells me in an aside, "That's our 'sleeping bunnies' song." She played this action song, in which the children pretend to sleep and then wake up and hop, and Sebastian joined happily, recovering from his dismay. She inserted his elephant idea into a script that she already possessed, substituting the word *elephant* for *bunnies* when singing. She set his idea within a predictable script that could be shared with the group. But Sebastian had more ideas. During the song, he said, "I want to be a sleeping dog," and Sonia, watching the video, said, "I was surprised here that he didn't get up and hop with everybody. He still was the dog [crawling] on the floor."

Here we see the child attempting to generate action scripts himself. In this second instance, his script, which differed from the group script, was tolerated, when, in contrast, his attempt to rejoin the group during the musical shape game was frustrated.

Sonia wanted to be spontaneous. It was not that she could not adjust her plan occasionally to absorb children's interests; it was more that she always called up a previously constructed teacher-centered script, culturally shared — something where the form was already given — and perhaps had no alternative for situations in which children generate their own scripts (as in play), make up their own songs or games. All she was missing, from the perspective of developmentally appropriate practice, was a frame, or script, for handing control back to the child. When Sebastian wanted to be an elephant, for instance, she could have said, "How could you be an elephant?" or "What does your elephant do? Do you want to show me?"

We live by scripts; they are essential for getting through the day. However, the scripts described above, and used especially in the construction of the teachers' weekly themes, were closed to much alteration or participation by the children, because they were conducted as teacher-centered activities in which the teacher's purposes were paramount. The teacher was in control, and the children's participation was predesigned, the answers known, the response closed-ended. There were few free moves and, without the chance of a free move, the children had no opportunity for choice, for decision making. Sebastian constantly attempted free moves, which were sometimes accepted and frequently corrected (he sat on the bench a lot). Does it really make a difference to the child whether there is much room made for his agenda? In Sebastian's case, after several months he stopped wanting to come to the program, and his mother withdrew him.

THE ROLE OF REFLECTION IN GENERATING NEW SCRIPTS

A key difference between developmentally appropriate practice and teacher dominion is the source of teacher evaluation of activity. In teacher-centered practice the source is the teacher's image of the pre-planned activity: if Jill planned a craft with a face for her toddlers, she was pleased when their products approximated faces. In a sense, the external activity in the real world serves the teacher's internal image; at least the image is the reference point. In contrast, in developmentally appropriate practice, the teacher serves not the concept of curriculum, but the child. She does not see herself as the dominant source of learning but rather assigns that role to the child's activity itself. Thus the source of evaluation of her own actions lies outside herself, in the response of the child, and this is why observation is the foundation of the practice. The teacher observes in order to decide what to do. This requires that she think, weigh her potential responses, before acting. If she is attending to the child, then it follows logically that since individuals are unique, the automaticity of responses can be broken. There are still automatic scripts for action, but they are of a different order, not so dependent on exact repetition and not dependent upon following her agenda alone. In her minutely calibrated adjustments of situations to children, there is complexity, variety, individual difference, and personalization. Reflection is a critical aspect of developmentally appropriate practice.

My ideas about reflection in professional practice are derived from Schön's (1983, 1987) conception of reflection-in-action as problem solving. In conducting a data search for evidence of reflection, I devised a criterion for determining whether an event was reflective, using his sense of the term. He talks of "surfacing" problems, bringing to bear all one's experience and beliefs crystallized around some "overarching theory" and, out of this, devising or generating potential solutions, which are enacted in action and evaluated according to the "backtalk" of the situation (Schön, 1987, p.158). The reflection has to be in terms of some principles, some theory of action, and it is either reflection or a script that connects theory and action. A new idea to try out in action is theory enacted, and it forms part of a teacher's practical knowledge.

To illustrate this point, here is Liz's reaction to the first time she provided laminated cutout cardboard telephones for the children as a support device when planning and reviewing activity. Each teacher sat at her snack table with five children, and the telephones invited a game of reviewing with the teacher the activities that each child had engaged in during the morning. Watching the video, Liz immediately said she would make more telephones; she "had enough for every teacher to have one, and one or two children [at the snack table] . . . but they all wanted one to hold" [L3.15]. Here we see the general principle of the High/Scope model—that children require their own materials in order to interact—implicitly inferred in her observation that each child at her table wanted material and she was thus obligated to provide it. It is when the principle or value is seen to be unmet that she is mobilized to act.

However, evaluation of activity—the surfacing of a problem—is insufficient as a criterion demonstrating reflection when using Schön's conception. Also present must be some idea for addressing the problem and some evidence of enacting this in practice. When Liz tells me she will make more phones, and I later observe a basket of these, I can see she has used reflection-in/on-action to affect her practice.

I searched the data set for each teacher for such instances, using as a criterion for reflection-in/on-action the surfacing of a problem, generating a potential solution, trying this out in the setting, and then assessing how it worked. For each participant there were at least three to six such situations. Then I wanted to know where such reflection-in/on-action occurred in relation to perpetuated scripts for action in the setting. For Sonia, Carla, and Jill, the examples of reflection-in/on-action that emerged occurred, without exception, within the process of carrying out teacher-centered scripts. They concerned either the content of the script and how to accomplish it, or the fitting together of routine and content. Here are several examples.

When Sonia played the musical shapes game, a modification of musical chairs, she realized in the midst of laying out her cutout shapes on the floor (for the children to sit on when the music stopped) that the children would probably jump or dive for the shapes, colliding with one another. Thus she altered the action of the game, in the process of describing it to the children, from walking around the shapes to crawling on the floor [S3.12, SV1].

Carla, in the midst of a craft to construct pumpkin masks, decided to permit her group of 11 to go to the bathroom individually as they finished their masks, rather than adhering to her normal practice of taking them en masse before group activity began [C1.10]. She did this because they had already started their masks, and she did not want to interrupt their activity to go to the bathroom.

With Nora and Liz the contexts in which reflection-in/on-action occurred were of a different character, addressing issues of the framework, the structure of how to do things. In the work of these two teachers old scripts were broken open and new ones generated. In the chapter on Nora we saw major change in her total disposition toward her work and one example of this change, beginning with her discomfort when boys did not like her crafts and the series of changes she made that altered her practical knowledge as a result. Here we will look at an instance of reflection-in/on-action as it occurred throughout Liz's work when I was present. Liz had problems with "sand going up to the housekeeping." She was in conflict, and a demonstrably uncomfortable conflict, with her perception of what should happen contradicting the reality before her. And like Nora, the consequences over months in time resulted in a change in her practical knowledge.

Reflection-in/on-Action and Change in Practical Knowledge: "Sand Going up to Housekeeping"

At my visit in December, Liz complained that "sand kept going up to housekeeping." This area for play about families and the processes they engage in was up a set of child-sized carpeted stairs in a triangular-shaped loft. It held a tiny wooden sink and stove, a cupboard, a box with clothes and purses and there was also an area with dolls and blankets and baby paraphernalia. There were two problems here. One was the children's insistence on transporting sand up to the loft to play, and the other was her perception that there was insufficient material in the area to promote their play. "Now that area is in dire need of some help" [L1.3]. Although she did not make this connection explicit, there was some implication that she felt the continuing trail of sand up to housekeeping day after day, in spite of her repeated requests that it stay in the sand area, was due to lack of materials in the area to satisfy their play and that she should provide these in some other way.

The difficulty with sand going upstairs to housekeeping was simply that the loft was carpeted, and the janitors complained continually that they couldn't get it out, there would be sand fleas. Most of the materials in Liz's room could be moved around freely by the children, and this was their expectation: the verbal instruction to keep sand in the sandbox was simply ineffective in limiting their activity. Watching the children truck their little pots of sand carefully up the stairs, I was reminded of how much very young children love to pile materials up, transport them somewhere, and dump them: we sometimes jokingly say of 2-year olds that they need a pile-and-dump curriculum.

Liz's first attempt to solve this problem was to provide more materials in housekeeping, a sort of distraction strategy that often works well with this age group. The student teacher who was assigned to "enhance" the area collected donations from parents, organized the area with labels for pots and pans, with milk cartons and dish detergent, "put in new shoes and new purses and some new clothes and we still don't have a crib but we have a box up there that's subbing as a crib which works wonderfully" [L4.1]. This was in February, and Liz still felt she "would like to see a lot more things up there" [L4.1], but she wanted to permit her student teacher to take the initiative.

By my third visit, in January, Liz had solved the sand problem. This difficulty bothered her sufficiently that she had discussed it with the consultants who coached her during her in-service, and the solution she found was to remove all the containers from the sand area and "put [in] things that sand goes right through" [L3.20]. She replaced the bowls and cups with sieves and funnels and tubes: the sand ran through the implement before the children could carry it anywhere and also focused their attention on a different process. This solved the problem effectively.

Or so Liz thought. Soon paint started to make its way upstairs. "They were taking paint containers and taking them upstairs and pouring them and making soup! And a lot of paint got on the carpet!" [L5.5]. While she had effectively stopped the problem with one material, these tiny children, ever-inventive, had found a substitute for carrying out this obviously satisfying process.

In reflecting on this problem and finding a solution, Liz returned to her theme of "not enough material" or attempting to meet their needs by providing materials that would suit their activity, a general belief of developmental appropriateness, and she set up a "gooey area" with "lots of activities with cooking pots and bowls and gooey substances and goop . . . pouring and mixing playdough with sand." She commented that "they need that obviously, and the kids are just loving it" [L5.5]. As the children poured and mashed, totally engrossed and generating a mess that would leave many teachers with their jaws stuck at their knees, there was no question of its success in drawing children into concentrated activity.

But housekeeping, still in February, continued to be a problem for Liz. "There aren't enough materials up there just yet," she told me, though

she had just added "new food," plastic apples and green peppers [L5.1].
She thought what was missing were more things to manipulate. This was
corroborated for her when we reviewed a video segment of children playing in the loft and Dryden shouted out, "Where's the plates?" When she
saw this on videotape, Liz said, "Gosh, I don't think I even heard him. He
cooked and he needed a plate. We really need to get together on that area.
. . . Isn't that sad! It's sad because he needed that material" [L5.4]. While
recognizing how she frames this problem, we also see her tremendous
commitment to providing the children with lots of materials, with everything they might think of to use.

In this same interview I asked her what her ideal setting would look
like. She offered a vivid and detailed description, including the following:

> Well, again, it's the housekeeping. More things for the housekeep-
> ing. . . . And I would move the housekeeping downstairs. I really
> like the loft idea, but I think the loft would be nice for a book corner.
> [L5.12]

This was in February, and mentioned almost as an aside. In April I
dropped in unexpectedly and briefly to say hello and Liz told me "housekeeping is coming downstairs, going right next to sand." By this point it
was a clear plan, and she had scheduled time when she and her colleague
could accomplish this. What is noteworthy is the fact that for such major
change it took 2 months for the idea to move from a casual statement to
the point where there was a plan for carrying out the idea. Because an
idea is present does not mean the vision of how to transform it into action
is also available: there is a design phase of altering present to desired
circumstance that accumulates and grows slowly.

In June I met with Liz for the long interview in which I offered
her the feedback paper describing what I saw as her personal practical
knowledge, garnered from what she said and did in her work setting. The
point was to give her an opportunity to clarify, refine, or comment on my
perceptions, both in writing and in conversation. During this interview
she told me they had moved housekeeping downstairs as planned in April,
with surprising and satisfying results.

> And you know what? There are hardly any materials in there at all!
> Remember me? We need more materials, we have to have more of
> this, more of that.
>
> *Yes! So what happened?*
> There are three pots, two muffin tins, like you saw the pegboard

with them seriated on there? Parents will bring in boxes with food stuffs, all that, just to leave it out for awhile. I like to encourage them to do that. And what else is in there, a stove and a sink.

So are you finding it doesn't need materials like you thought it did? What happened there?
No, no. Well block play came in and sand play came in and water, so they're representing the things with those and they don't need the stuff I fretted over! There's less in there, less, a lot less, and it works great. It works fine. . . . Oh the play's more imaginative. They're using, [gestures] "this is going to be this and this is something else." A lot of representation. When I brought down all the materials that were in housekeeping, Bess and I brought them down, there wasn't enough room for everything we had there. Like we lost quite a bit of shelf space. And I said, let's just take it all out, and leave the basics here. They're using it really, really well. You know, beads are popcorn, things are this and things are that, it's great.

So you didn't need plates after all!
No, we didn't need plates. Who needs plates! This block is a plate, and this block standing up this way is a cup! [L6.17–18]

Liz removed housekeeping from the problematic carpet, brought it down into the busiest area of the classroom, adjacent to sand, and permitted children to interchange materials from one area to another. At first she worried because she had provided fewer materials than in the loft, and then she found the area working superbly with less, once the children could readily bring items from other areas. This had the added benefit of generating play that was more imaginative. Lack of material resources for housekeeping, as a problem, dissolved, and the tension over the movement of sand was preempted by bringing the two areas into poximity, permitting the actions, the interest that the carpet had led her to correct. And in the process of meeting the children's need, saving the carpet, and reducing the tensions from this problem, she had transformed her own image of what it was necessary to provide in this favorite play area of the children. This, I submit, is a series of reflections-in/on-action, a series of unique solutions to problems that had been a major source of tension for the duration of the period I was working with Liz.

It is also an example of the degree of change in Liz's room, the sense that there is continuous flux as small adjustments are tried out. I have described only the houskeeping area, but there were continual small changes in other areas as well. There was a dynamic quality to her room, a sense of alertness to possibility, a tendency to interpret the actions of children as expressing need, and a willingness to search out the intention and meet it, in part, by adjusting the physical environment.

THE RELATION OF SCRIPTS, REFLECTION, AND PRACTICAL KNOWLEDGE

Reflection-in/on-action occurs in situations when there is something (whether just at the moment or long term) that the teacher anticipates or decides does not work quite as she might wish. There is some conflict facing her. In other words, at least two things have to be present for reflection to occur: some consciously articulated segment of theory or value or way of doing something, on the one hand, and a mismatch with the current reality on the other. Nora's boys did not like her crafts. Liz's children took paint and sand to housekeeping. Without the internal image or vision, there can be no evaluation of the lived experience before her. She cannot reflect unless she holds some image in consciousness that mirrors something in experience. It is when they do not match that the teacher is irritated, bothered, mobilized to generate something new in the situation.

Put in Schön's terms, she needs an overarching theory or appreciation system with which to compare lived reality. Clearly, the framework of developmentally appropriate practice provides one such appreciation system for teachers, for it articulates a coherent set of values, beliefs, images, and procedures for constructing such practice. Liz was the only teacher to say she was attempting to implement developmentally appropriate practice when asked to choose from a list a model of practice like her own [L6.15]. The other teachers chose two models, schooling practice and developmentally appropriate practice, or schooling and play group models [N6.9; J6.3; C6.17; S7.7], and by these choices they demonstrated the existence of at least two appreciation systems that oriented their work.

But there is another problem here, and that is the previously described distinction between conscious, purposeful knowing (the focus on the head of the nail, in Polanyi's example) and tacit, or inarticulate, knowledge (all the subsidiary skills necessary in holding, lifting, and successfuly hitting that nail on its head). I argue that the teacher cannot reflect upon the knowledge she uses in performance unless she has articulated it, that tacit knowledge is not accessible to reflection-*on*-action until something occurs to bring it up as something to consider. Let me explain by using the analogy of figure–ground relations. Nelson (1977), for instance, in examining acquisition of concepts in children, sees scripts for action as offering a frame or ground, and the concept as a figure that fits it. What the teacher consciously reflects upon has to be lifted out as the figure, and all the knowing-that and knowing-how that the figure subsumes is ground or background.

The way that Carla, Sonia, and Jill used teacher-centered activity (including themes, large-group process, and fixed time schedules) can be interpreted using this analogy of figure–ground relations. Themes, as they were used by these teachers, had a spatial and temporal script adapted from conventional schooling, and this formed a ground of expectations, a frame for the activity. The concepts that the teacher selected out and consciously thought about as her program material became the figure. Sonia, for example, thought about how her theme shapes — triangle, square, circle — would fit her scripted routines for circle and craft. When I gave the examples of reflection-in-action for Sonia, Carla, and Jill, I noted that they occurred within teacher-centered scripts for a specific activity and time frame. They did not think about the frame or ground in which they were offered. The teacher thought about the figure, the part she could distinguish.

To make clear the analogy of the figure–ground distinction to conscious and tacit knowing, think back to the theme planning of Sonia, Carla, and Jill. Carla answered all questions about what she was trying to do, about the structure of her program, in terms of the specific content that she wished to convey around a theme — different smells or tools, a description of objects, a focus on red. She could not understand my questions about how it was done: that was beyond the figure consciously planned and held in her mind. Yet, tacitly, she knew how to conduct theme content in a structure supporting teacher dominion, for she performed it daily with aplomb.

Another example of this taken-for-granted ground around theme and time was Jill's comment that she could not use the African games brought in by a parent during the Africa theme because they arrived on Thursday. In other words, the time for Africa was almost gone. When weekly themes were scripts for program, the use of time was so automatic that the ways in which this use constricted activity simply did not surface.

However, Liz and Nora could also think about the ground, or, to put it another way, they had somehow surfaced the scripts or frames for action as a landscape for reflection. In other words, the knowledge that was tacit for the others became articulable and conscious for Nora and Liz. How might this be so? Clearly one of the values of the High/Scope in-service for Liz was that it taught her different scripts, such as a script for planning and reviewing the activity of children with them, and a script for conducting small-group activities in a non-teacher-centered fashion. The process of learning two possibilities, two formats or frames, could be responsible for permitting the teacher to see that the frame exists to be thought about.

But then what of the other teachers, who were caught between two frameworks for action in day care, tolerating these without appearing to resolve or even notice the tensions that were surfaced by Nora? Jill, Carla, and Sonia slid back and forth between scripts for teacher dominion and moments of developmental appropriateness toward individuals in a kind of balancing act or stasis, without much change, beyond the decision to tip one way or the other in a specific instance. Somehow the tension had not surfaced as problematic. It was taken for granted, part of the practical knowledge the teacher brought to her work. This was the unreflective portion, while her energy was absorbed with the content for these respective teacher-directed or play scripts.

Part of what was missing, I submit, was a sufficiently powerful image or appreciation system that would permit the teacher to lift out scripts or patterns of action as problematic. Where does such an appreciation system come from? There are several possible sources. It can come from the teacher or it can come from the institution, as it did in both Nora's and Liz's cases. The adoption by centers of a unifying theory or framework, such as High/Scope or curriculum webs in these cases, appeared to free teachers who had previously used teacher-centered processes to think in new ways. Alternatively, if a teacher consciously recognizes two ways of doing something, she has the opportunity to make a choice and to reflect upon why that choice is appropriate.

Reflection-in/on-action can only occur within the parameters of what one knows. It is of necessity bounded by a teacher's theories-of-action, whether these are conscious, intentional, and perhaps planned, or whether they are tacit and automatic, occasioned in taken-for-granted scripts. What a teacher knows provides the horizon of her vision, in Greene's (1988) metaphor, her sense of the possibilities. What she does not know is beyond the horizon and cannot be thought about.

But there is a paradox here. Schön insists that reflection-in-action is full of tacit knowledge, knowing that is taken for granted, and while I understand his sense of that, I notice something else occurring with the participants in this research. If we examine the place where reflection *on* action occurs (for instance, words communicated to a researcher), it can only occur around something that has been lifted out of the stream of experience, something made conscious. What is tacit, automatic, cannot be openly reflected upon. Yet this is precisely what must be done for teachers to reflect fully upon their work. In order for reflection-on-action to occur concerning largely tacit, taken-for-granted scripts, the figure–ground relationship has to be broadened or reversed to bring into relief those taken-for-granted scripts as something that can be thought about.

How can this be done? There are two examples in this book illuminating how this occurred, for Liz and for Nora. In both cases, it was a tension or conflict experienced by the teacher that set in motion a process whereby the script that she had tacitly used became a forum for conscious reflection. For Liz it was initially an image–reality conflict, in that what she wanted from the housekeeping area was not occurring. The children's need to tote materials around conflicted with conventional use of the room, and this set in motion a series of problem-solving attempts. For Nora, the conflict was an image–reality one, too, for her previously successful crafts were disdained and she was disappointed. Internal conflict is not easy for teachers to tolerate: it comes with heavy emotional baggage. But what these examples suggest is that conflict perceived by the teacher is one route to making evident an arena where she has the power to change something so that it suits her better. It suggests that teachers should not fear points of conflict but accept them as arenas where interesting events can occur. The conflict is like a signpost, a literal "figure" in her personal landscape, which she can use as a mobilizer. At the points of conflict lie the routes to change.

It is interesting to note that in some places, conflict is used to mobilize teachers. Openness to moments of conflict in teaching is embraced by the Reggio Emilia approach to early education (Edwards et al., 1993). Preschool teachers in this Italian municipality are encouraged to discuss differences together, to confront their points of tension and disagreement as a route to expanding the boundaries of their thinking and practice; conflict is understood as a way to promote this. This is supported by their administration through expectations for both documentation of children's progress and frequent meetings to discuss their work.

I speculate that as teachers move toward more developmentally appropriate practice, reflection-in/on-action increases. This is possible for several reasons. First, the emphasis on observation and problem-solving skills, as well as on individual uniqueness, may assist the construction of a disposition toward a richer, more varied, and more flexible practice. Second, a more relaxed use of time and the sanctioning of considerably more child-initiated activity offer possibilities for evaluating events outside the teacher: she has given up total control of content and so has mental space to think about what children are doing.

9 | The Frameworks as Public and Private Domains

When I started research with these teachers, I wanted to understand what made it so difficult for them to construct developmentally appropriate practice in early childhood settings and thus, in part, why I felt so limited as a teacher educator when the practice that I hoped to help them construct so seldom appeared full blown. By the end of the study I understood that teaching is much more conflicted and complex than I had previously realized, even in my years as an early childhood educator, that I, too, had been guilty of thinking I could transform practice merely by injecting the theory of developmentally appropriate practice into students: I have understood that that is one of the myths of teacher education. But now I can see that it is more difficult than I thought even during my study — and my experience substituting for a week in day care impressed this more forcefully than any amount of research could have done — for the teacher continuously negotiates her way through an intense multiple agenda in which, using all her values, feelings, perceptions, and beliefs, all aspects of her practical knowledge, she must quickly judge and choose the most productive, the "right thing to do" for the immediate moment.

In this chapter I wish to return to the concerns of Chapter 1, summarize the case studies in terms of scripts for action and reflection-in/on-action in practical knowledge, comment on systemic constraints, and briefly address limitations of the frameworks, particularly those of developmentally appropriate practice. Finally, I will comment on notions of public and private domains in early childhood settings.

SUMMARY OF THE FIVE CASES

Thinking of how each teacher was situated with regard to the frameworks under discussion, we see that Liz was the sole teacher to display a clear and conscious commitment to a single framework, and to act in her teaching in a way that both she and others identified with the framework of developmentally appropriate practice. She viewed the first 7 years of her teaching as following teacher dominion: 2 years later she had rejected this.

Nora, we saw, was in the beginning phases of change; this was not directly apparent during the first 5 months of data generation but revealed at our final interview 2 months later: she was negotiating her way from teacher dominion toward more developmentally appropriate practice. Jill was admittedly comfortable with both frameworks, knew both quite well, and seemed equally committed to both in her practice, though several comments in her final interview suggested seeds of change favoring developmental appropriateness. Carla's conscious practice favored a developmental approach, but this was present in her setting in brief, atypical moments directed toward individual children, whereas the bulk of her practice was teacher-centered. This framework for practice was tacit, taken for granted as normal, and not readily surfaced for discussion between us. Sonia's practice, too, was primarily teacher-centered, but in our final interview she revealed a longing for a more developmental approach, which she did indeed display in occasional moments of practice. Each teacher's story with respect to the two frameworks for practice is unique to her personal history and to the point in time when this research was conducted. Yet even as we acknowledge the unique aspects, we can also see that what is common among them is the necessity of responding in some fashion to both frameworks: they are present both in settings and in the mythic expectations that surround early childhood work. Teachers cannot avoid them. They must negotiate their way through both forms of practice, coping with the conflicts, incongruities, anxieties, and stress that their simultaneous presence guarantees.

Let's briefly summarize each teacher's location in the conflict between the two frameworks in relation to her scripts for action and her reflection-in/on-action.

Sonia was locked into teacher-centered scripts for action that were automatic, taken-for-granted practice which she, in our final interview, showed herself unable to surmount at that time. She was aware of a more developmentally appropriate approach, describing it as "being spontaneous" and "following the child's lead," which she acknowledged she did not know how to do but which occurred quite spontaneously in rare moments when she was not handcuffed to a teacher-centered script. However, her desire to be an elementary school teacher should not be forgotten. Implicitly, she valued both frameworks for practice, favoring teacher dominion in her practice but developmental appropriateness in her talks with me. Her final interview revealed her dissatisfaction with how she was negotiating these two frameworks in practice. Nor should the overwhelming systemic constraints in her practice be forgotten, for the very schedule and numbers of children coming and going in her room *assumed* a framework of teacher dominion. Reflection-in/on-action occurred as tiny moments in practice coupled with general reflectiveness in our interviews: that she managed even this, given the press of things to do, was remarkable, for the setting neither suggested nor supported teacher reflection.

Carla, too, was locked into the framework of teacher dominion, through structured practices that were in place in the setting and preferred by center policy: the director did not believe "middle-class methods" were effective with the children. However, somewhat to my surprise, Carla also valorized developmentally appropriate practice and insisted that her practice displayed this, giving examples that fit this framework and denying her teacher-centered practice. Like Sonia, she inserted developmentally appropriate practice into broader scripts for teacher-centered practice as atypical resolutions to momentary dilemmas favoring individual children, and she saw herself as doing this more than other teachers in the setting. The moments of reflection-in/on-action that emerged in her practice were *within* broader scripts for teacher dominion, such as offering one more rock to paint when children enjoyed and wanted more of this activity. Teacher-centered scripts themselves could not be easily surfaced as something to discuss and were assumed as the normal bedrock of practice. This, I argue, is to be expected and is exacerbated by conditions of work that intensify and multiply work processes, as was the case for Carla.

Nora had come from 5 years of work experience using teacher-centered practice, an experience with which she was dissatisfied, into a setting where developmentally appropriate practice was more favored. As she experienced using scripts for action that were different from the ones she had known — such as a flexible schedule, an intact group of children, patterns of helping children make choices in the room — she began to value these more, to identify with them and prefer them. By the end of the year, she had identified major points of change in both her value system and her practice. In particular, her ability to observe children at play, taking into account their needs and interests and controlling her own response accordingly (as she did when a 2-year-old painted the skin of her hand, or Orlando and Raphael produced a storm in water play), showed her awareness and adoption of new scripts for action favoring developmental appropriateness. By the time of our final interview, she was shifting allegiance from teacher dominion to developmental appropriateness and she was aware of specific practices, scripts for action, which she was mastering that enabled her to favor one framework over the other. In terms of reflection-in/on-action, she was also beginning to be dissatisfied with previous teacher-dominated scripts that shut down children's play, such as closing the block area when the children pinched their fingers playing firefighters, and to search with her colleague for more developmentally appropriate solutions. During our time together her practice was in flux, unstable, undergoing rapid change, although this would not have been apparent if I had not gone back with the feedback paper 2 months after the initial 5 months of data generation.

Of the five teachers, Jill's practice was most evenly split between teacher dominion and developmental appropriateness. The scripts for action in her setting favored teacher dominion in the organization of time and routine, but even where this was not necessary, she and her colleague continued in the classroom with a highly routinized, fixed schedule with specific activities slotted into brief periods. However, her observation of individual children's needs and interests was well developed, and she responded to these even in group activity, transforming several formerly teacher-centered scripts for action, such as show and tell, into small-group activities in which children could initiate action and play with materials. Her practice swung back and forth, with her allegiance to both frameworks quite strong, and she acknowledged this in responding to the feedback paper. In fact, it was in her practice where I first could see how the teacher could be caught with two major value systems that conflicted and how she worked in practice to negotiate her way between them. Jill's reflection-in/on-action occurred both in moments of practice with individuals and around entire scripts for practice (such as how to alter cooking or how to engage children in using library books after story circle). Yet in spite of small changes she had made at the time of our final interview that clearly favored developmentally appropriate practice, the rigid time structure in place in the setting and her preference for teacher-centered theme content such as shapes, colors, and numbers gave the impression of a practice in stasis—while we were meeting at least.

Liz, during the research period, had consolidated developmentally appropriate practice after an intense in-service and a period of active rejection of her former teacher-centered practice in early childhood. This was supported in her setting by administrative policies such as weekly planning time and consultants who visited her program to discuss progress with her. The developmentally appropriate scripts that she used were different from the practice of teacher dominion in almost all respects; for instance, to encourage language development in her 2- and 3-year-olds, instead of focusing attention on listening skills and attentiveness to group process, as did Jill, she used a running commentary to describe their actions back to them and encouraged the language in which they described their own activity. Whether by temperament, by training, or because she worked (like Carla) with challenging children at educational risk—or the interaction of these—she continuously was framing problems and trying out solutions for them; these solutions involved not simply moments of practice but the generation of new scripts for action in organizing the environment. Liz was the sole teacher who had broken the hold of the concept of time as it is structured in teacher-centered practice (although Nora was aware of the difference because her colleague had accomplished this as well).

I argue that in frameworks of practice for teacher dominion the handling of time as scarce, finite, and to be used for segmented activity is the aspect most taken for granted and most difficult to surface as problematic. Oddly, the only way I know to break this hegemony of time organization is to focus attention on the organization of space, to make changes in the environment and watch children's responses, and, in the process, to let time go, let it vary rather than holding it constant, something I first learned when I was in training as a Montessori teacher.

Reflection-in/on-action is an active process in which the teacher has agency, the same sort of agency she encourages children to experience in initiating a plan, carrying it through, and assessing the result in developmentally appropriate practice. It makes both children and adults inquirers, problem solvers, people in the midst of wrestling with the material of their lives. Conflict is a major component of this, conflict between belief and reality, beliefs in contrasting frameworks, between teacher and teacher, teacher and child. The importance of conflict in promoting reflection is recognized by the Reggio Emilia approach, which actively promotes it in teacher discussions (Edwards et al., 1993). Perhaps, then, it is not surprising that more reflection-in/on-action occurs as teachers move toward practice that is more developmentally appropriate. Whereas agency in teacher dominion is used primarily to plan and to control children, it is used in developmentally appropriate practice to observe and respond, to match intent to child need, to discover and uncover.

Perhaps it is also not unusual that more reflection-in/on-action occurs where there is more center support for it in practices such as freeing teacher time for planning, discussing, and documenting program.

> There is little institutional emphasis on teachers reflecting about their goals and objectives, about their teaching strategies, or their children's progress. Neither self-study — using diaries, case studies, or anecdotal records — nor collaborative reflection — using staff meetings, case consultation, and supervisory feedback and problem solving conferences — is valued highly by most schools and centers. (Bowman & Stott, 1994, p. 129)

Yet it is precisely the carving out of time for just this sort of reflection that is necessary if teachers are to gain a sense of agency in teaching and of mastery of their own work. Without administrative support, this reflection simply won't happen. And as we saw, when the work processes of teachers are intensified by pressing multiple agendas, reflection becomes impossible: in Sonia's case we saw the result as a longing for a practice she does not know how to fulfill; in Carla's case we saw a denial of aspects of practice and an attempt to valorize less typical moments.

SYSTEMIC CONSTRAINTS

If we think of the early childhood teacher as a contested site for the location of teacher-centered practice or developmentally appropriate practice, we can accept the tension and the difficulty she faces as she chooses to act moment to moment in her teaching world. While those of us who are teacher educators might desire that her practice be solely developmentally appropriate or teacher-centered, the teacher is caught in a network of systemic constraints that favor one or the other practice. The extent and severity of systemic constraints that shaped teachers' practice varied considerably among the five participants, but this is not the place to attempt a full articulation of their impact. However, this impact cannot go unacknowledged. Whereas, in general, space was not an insurmountable constraint in that teacher needs were met on the whole, the organization of time was a powerful constraint.

In the three cases in which time was organized as a fixed schedule of activities that had to be followed, teachers were rushed, harassed by too much to do in too little time, their work processes uncomfortably intensified. This was exacerbated where the numbers of children were high and, in Sonia's case, where she was juggling several programs. As well, these teachers — Sonia, Carla, Jill — were unaware that they were taking for granted this organization of time, that its very automaticity as normal precluded them from questioning it or thinking there could be other possibilities for time organization in early childhood contexts. Liz and Nora had experienced other possible organizations of time and preferred them, and because they were less harassed by immediate pressures to act, they were also more able to reflect on their practice. Where intensification of work processes was severe, as in Sonia's case, there were actual physical symptoms of stress (pounding headaches, for instance), which indicated extreme tension. It is probably no coincidence that Carla and Sonia were the least reflective in their practice (at least in terms of what emerged in the data generated by research), for the intensity resulting from the numbers of children and programs and the rigid time organization in their practice left them with no option but a rapid undertaking of the next item on the agenda for action. Constant busyness precludes reflection: mental space is totally absorbed. If teacher educators, supervisors, and administrators want teachers in early childhood to think about what they are doing, to engage in a conscious practice, whether teacher-centered or developmentally appropriate, they must provide adequate time for reflective discussion and documentation, and they must reduce systemic constraints that intensify work beyond the bearable. Since the teacher will take up whatever is required as part of maintaining a professional stance, the burden is on administrators and those who fund early childhood settings to address systemic constraints.

LIMITATIONS OF THE FRAMEWORKS

I wish here merely to remind the reader of the extensive criticisms that teacher dominion has garnered and to focus primarily on developmentally appropriate practice. Teacher dominion has been widely critiqued in our society for the passivity and lack of agency it engenders (Jackson, 1968/1990), the submissiveness to labor-market demands that it requires (Giroux, Penna, & Pinar, 1981), and the depression and stress it causes in children (Burts, Hart, Charlesworth, & Kirk, 1990). It is critiqued for reproducing cultural conditions it nominally purports to correct [see, for instance, Anyon (1981)]. Its atomistic and mechanistic approach is deeply alienating to human endeavor and makes children feel they are waiting to live their lives. As Britzman (1991) says of the fragmentation of time in schools:

> Fragmented experience is the shattering of experience into discrete and arbitrary units that are somehow dissociated from all that made experience in the first place. It is experience that is less than it could be, because fragmented experience cannot be extended or transformed. This form of fragmentation separates knowledge from experience and experience from knower. (p. 35)

The very presence of developmentally appropriate practice is an implied critique of teacher dominion, a resistance to a world view that gives only the adult agency and sees learning as a one-way transmission. However, in the years following its initial articulation, developmentally appropriate practice has been widely critiqued and I wish to acknowledge this here. The data for the work of the teachers described in this book was generated in 1989–1990. Recognizing this point in time helps to situate the data and my interpretations of it in that period of fresh confidence following the ratification and publication of the position statement on developmentally appropriate practice in early childhood programs serving children from birth through age 8 (Bredekamp, 1987). Those of us with an allegiance to this practice believed we had, for the first time, entered a public, professional discourse through the broadcasting of a shared, standard description of practice that nevertheless was tolerant of broad differences. That our personal interpretations of this ideology could vary considerably was no deterrent to our sense of debut, of coming of age in the broader community of education across North America.

Since then criticisms of this initial pronouncement (Kessler, 1991; Mallory & New, 1994; Reifel, 1993) have prompted reassessments, refinements, and reconsiderations of the statements in an attempt to describe developmentally appropriate practice as its limitations have become clearer to divergent audiences (Bredekamp & Rosegrant, 1992). There are two principal limitations that these recent critiques address. The statements of guidelines are seen to fall into the trend of the dominant society to project norms onto all children, norms seen as universal ["DAP is for all children"—Bredekamp & Rosegrant (1992, p. 5)] but reflecting only dominant Eurocentric culture (Lubeck, 1994). This blindness with respect to other cultural norms and values stems from an overreliance on developmental psychology and a lack of attention to the role that culture plays in development (Bowman & Stott, 1994; New, 1994; C. B. Phillips, 1994; Williams, 1994). Second, the statements have been critiqued for lack of inclusion of a range of practices, such as direct instruction (though this is seen by adherents as a misunderstanding), considered necessary to provide appropriate education to some groups. These groups include the differently abled (Atwater, Carta, Schwartz, & McConnell, 1994) and groups representing the increasing cultural and racial diversity within North America (Bowman & Stott, 1994; C. B. Phillips, 1994; Williams, 1994). I will give examples of the arguments constructed and briefly indicate how these are being addressed.

Bowman and Stott (1994), for instance, see two aspects of the developmental theory on which developmentally appropriate practice is based as problematic because of the discipline's Eurocentric bias. The first difficulty is the assumption that principles of development are universal, whereas in cross-cultural studies (see Heath, 1983; New, 1993) well-documented differences are reported. The second difficulty is the assumption that intelligence is independent of culture. They show in a persuasive way how African American children negotiate their way between one culture in the family and another when they enter school, the contradictory requirements of each culture, and how some children make an allegiance to one (either family or school) at the expense of the other, while others manage somehow to negotiate successfully the requirements of each culture. What is clear is that lived life is more complex for these children, for they do not interact in a single homogenous culture. As New (1994) says, "developmental processes conform to contextual demands, including cultural values as well as socioeconomic circumstances, such that the very concept of optimal development appears negotiable" (p. 71).

It was not the intention of the position statement to exclude other cultures, for it was conceived as a broad statement of consensus within a diverse society. The critiques reveal blind spots. Situated within a culture, its members cannot see how their thought imposes on others: it is only those outside who can see the contrast between their lived reality and the prescription of the dominant society. Lubeck (1994) is, I think, incorrect to assert that these voices are silenced or that "there is no recognition that competing views [of practice] exist" (p. 36). There has been animated debate and a renegotiation process marked by the appearance of curriculum guidelines (Bredekamp & Rosegrant, 1992) to address precisely these issues.

Atwater and associates (1994), while noting many sources of agreement between developmentally appropriate practice and early childhood special education (for instance, the need for individualizing education, the importance to motivation of child-initiated activities), note three features of special education that are not standards of practice as the position statement describes. These are the need for "relatively structured instruction to achieve important goals" (p. 190), specific preparation for the next environment the child will enter, and outcomes-based monitoring and assessment. They believe there is room to broaden the guidelines to include use of these strategies. They can see these fitting within the broader context of embedding instruction in active engagement, employing a "least to most intrusive" (p. 194) strategy in intervention and an ecological approach that adjusts the environment to ensure child success.

Lubeck (1994) argues that the guidelines are universalist and overstate "their applicability and importance" (p. 30) and that they are authoritarian in structure, in that they assert best practices that are to be conveyed to teachers and parents, rendering parents as clients, recipients of professional expertise. What this does is to reduce parents to consumers rather than active participants in their child's education. What is missing in such arguments is the recognition that all professions operate in the dominant society by gaining status through the possession of a specialized body of knowledge not held by outsiders to the profession (Schön, 1983). The debate thus is in part a clash between the impetus for recognition of early childhood education as a profession, like medicine or law or architecture, and the impetus for recognition and status of the culturally and racially diverse groups with which dominant groups share early childhood settings.

A subtheme in this debate is the interest in developing a slightly reframed role for the teacher in early childhood. While teachers have long been viewed as constructivists in terms of their understandings of teaching (Duckworth, 1987; Kamii & DeVries, 1972), the sense of the teacher as an inquirer, as one who can teach in part using her own discoveries, has received additional impetus from the excitement generated by dissemination of the Reggio Emilia approach (Edwards et al., 1993), in which the teacher is simultaneously classroom ethnographer (documenting children's work through photographs, slides, videos, and transcripts of child language that are then shared with parents, children, and teachers), anthropologist (searching out the child's niche in family and community), and reflective practitioner (examining her teaching strategies with other teachers) (New, 1993). There is the growing sense that developmentally appropriate practice is too narrowly focused on children and should take into account the lives and development of all the adults around children — teachers, parents, cooks, janitors, and so forth (Jones, 1993; New, 1993; Wien, 1991). This is exciting for those of us participating in the field, for it suggests several ways of pulling ourselves out of the rigid teacher-centered scripts for action perpetuated merely because they are lived practices.

Another criticism of developmentally appropriate practice concerns the relation of the child to the community. The way developmentally appropriate practice is framed, the focus is on the individual child and his or her development, not the functioning of the group. In prioritizing the development of the individual child, the ideology reduces the importance of social organization, the handling of life in the group. It is, then, narrow in scope. A tight focus is, of course, a strength, for it gives clear direction, but it also leaves teachers to fend for themselves in developing ways of tolerating so much individualism within group life.

Unless group life is adequately managed, there can be no attention to individual activity within it (Wien, 1991). Teachers must first attend to the life of the community, such as whether everyone has a suitable activity. For instance, among the five teachers described here, rationales for activity did not simply take into account the needs of children's development. Rationales could be purely pragmatic, having such managerial purposes as moving children from one location to another. Jill, for instance, spread materials out on tables as children were leaving group activity and invited children to use them. She said that this aided in spreading the children evenly over the room. She told children where to sit in group contexts, seating quiet ones interspersed with noisy ones to prevent disrup-

tion. My point is that the focus of the ideology on the individual is insufficient to describe the totality of teacher practice. Realistically, it cannot
address the totality, but, like a language, provides a set of rules, a gram-
mar, by which situations can be recognized and a corresponding response
offered. The ideology as described is narrow in scope in that it does not
address the social group or the scripts for practice that serve the whole
group in developmentally appropriate ways.

THE RELATION OF TEACHER DOMINION AND DEVELOPMENTAL APPROPRIATENESS TO PUBLIC AND PRIVATE DOMAINS

Recently a student in practicum in an Ontario school complained that
when she worked in day care within a school setting children called her
"Deborah," but when she worked down the hall in their junior kindergarten class the same children called her "Miss Newman." This contrast in use
of address symbolizes not only society's different conceptions of the location of each of these settings but the fact that they are considered separate,
even when their physical presence occurs within the same building. The
difference in location is the public versus the private domain.

The elementary school is, in our society, the first institution into
which the young child steps that is conceived as a public domain where
children will function without family. (Hospitals don't count because
there the child's illness is served and there are no requirements for willed
action on the child's part.) However, in the public school, for the first
time in the child's life, there are specific, detailed requirements for how
the child is to match his or her actions to the expectations of the setting.
How the child manages to do this matters very much both to teachers and
to parents. Distinct from church or shopping, which are other public
domains entered by young children, they enter school alone as a representative of their family and community, and they are expected to function
independently of their parents. The fact that school is a public domain is
symbolized in such actions as the differential address used: teachers call
children by their given name, but children address teachers using a title
and surname. This symbolizes in part that the teacher is a representative
of the institution of schooling and that the child is to interact with the
teacher in ways specified by the authority vested in her role, however she
defines it. The scripts for action for teacher dominion—from roll call to
opening exercises (such as the ubiquitous "calendar") to organization of
activity areas—presuppose the teacher's authority to determine and shape
children's actions.

In contrast, in the early childhood setting, these very same children address the adults around them by their given names. This is viewed as a situation of reciprocity, a marker of a personal relationship between caregiver and child in which each is known personally, that is, as a distinctive human in relationship with another distinctive human. This form of address is a symbol for the fact that the early childhood setting is imagined as a private domain for children, likened to the family. The concept of family care and of personal relationship informs the setting because of the strong need for nurturing associated with adequate development of young children: stylized, stereotyped interactions in which children take on roles before they have even developed a concept of a role in play (Bateson, 1971) are seen to be inappropriate and limiting.

In passing I wish to acknowledge that as work processes in our society have become intensified by, among other things, technological advances and the pressure upon institutions of education to service these advances, and as the economic pressures upon women to join the labor force in the past 30 years have steadily increased, personal life has eroded. Illich (1983) predicted that home life would deteriorate until it was like our use of gas stations, merely a place where basic needs are restocked while all other time is spent in work. That this is detrimental to children in the extreme is recognized (see, for example, Leach, 1994).

Early childhood settings may be, outside the life of the family, one of the few remaining contexts of social life in which space is made for the personal. Most institutionalized contexts — schools, hospitals, stores, universities, offices — remove the personal, and personal difference, from the stereotyped patterns of functioning that serve to perpetuate these institutions: their scripts require compliance to institutional purposes. Teacher dominion requires this, too, and can be seen as training for future roles in institutions. Developmentally appropriate practice, on the other hand, permits the personal, the unique qualities of individuals, to shine forth, both in creative production (paintings, block structures and sand arrangements, stories and books, and inquiry about the world) and in genuine interactions with others. It leaves room for joy among adults and children, and the very real affection that grows out of knowing others as they are.

Developmentally appropriate practice insists, in the interests of children's development, that early childhood is still a private domain, a place for personal life, not a public one, and it stresses family and community values. I think part of the tension for teachers in early childhood settings between teacher-centered practice and developmentally appropriate practice is that, however the practice occurred, many settings in which they work adopted teacher-centered practices to shape their organization of children in groups, adopted them in a straightforward way from what was known and experienced about schools. These practices are largely taken-for-granted scripts for action that are difficult for teachers to surface as problematic. When they value developmentally appropriate practice, their practices in this framework may simply be a weak overlay, directed at individual children, on top of scripts for teacher dominion, and the contradictions in practice are not noticed. They also see themselves as operating in developmentally appropriate ways, and in part they are. What they cannot see is that the public, institutionalized style of these scripts for action in which they are caught undercut developmentally appropriate practice. So, to summarize, practices used in the public domain of elementary schooling have been adopted in the private domain of early childhood, and the ways in which this is incompatible with developmentally appropriate practice are invisible.

WHAT CAN WE DO?

It is impossible to emerge from a research project such as this, and the reworking and rewriting several years later that are necessary to produce a book, without being changed by the process. One of the lessons I have learned is to let go of the frustration I used to feel at the limited extent to which I seemed capable of encouraging the transformation of practice toward developmental appropriateness and to let go of my previous sense that it was somehow the teachers' fault for not producing this more. I hope the reader has gained some sense of the ways this may be very difficult for individual teachers. Unless she enters a situation in which developmentally appropriate practice is already well constructed, she quickly adopts the scripts for practice for other frameworks already in place in the setting. These frequently reflect teacher-centered practice, unless someone has consciously adopted and supported another framework for practice. Unless supportive structures are provided by her administration, there will be no time for her to think about her practice, to bring some problems to the surface to address consciously and to share with others.

Teachers' work is conflicted, contradictory, muddied, and torn by myriad demands of a dynamic lived life in which each teacher must negotiate her way, shaping small moments as she is shaped by the very things she takes most for granted — especially conceptions of use of time. The demands upon her for performance, for action, generate a level of busyness that is scarcely conceivable to those who have not taught in classrooms. Teachers' work is extraordinarily difficult and challenging.

Those of us who hope to support the work of teachers (administrators, curriculum consultants, practicum supervisors, teacher educators, and so forth) can help in several ways, beyond simply a better understanding of the context of teacher work in early childhood. Like the support given to teachers in Reggio Emilia (Edwards et al., 1993; New, 1993), we can work to change systemic constraints so that time is opened up for reflection, for review of practice, for the surfacing of incipient conflicts that the teacher senses but has not had time to address. We can encourage the reflective process by giving teachers opportunities to document children's activity and the development of their curriculum, encourage them to make changes that they themselves generate, to try out solutions to self-set problems of teaching. Rather than appearing merely as experts with authoritative knowledge, we can encourage their sense of mastery over their work, their sense of agency. Ultimately we must trust teachers to develop the worlds of teaching in which they work, recognizing that their negotiations through two common frameworks for action, teacher dominion and developmental appropriateness, are conflicted, frequently contradictory, stressful, exciting, and challenging and that the agency that they can develop in taking action in early childhood settings is ultimately a preferred way to model for children the process of coming to life, of living in a shared social world of responsibility, of care for others and love of life itself.

References

Anyon, Jean. 1981. Social class and the hidden curriculum of work. In Henry Giroux, Anthony Penna, & William Pinar (Eds.), *Curriculum and instruction* (pp. 317–341). Berkeley, CA: McCutchan.

Apple, Michael. 1979. *Ideology and curriculum*. London: Routledge & Kegan Paul.

Atwater, Jane, Judith Carta, Ilene Schwartz, & Scott McConnell. 1994. Blending developmentally appropriate practice and early childhood special education: Redefining best practice to meet the needs of all children. In Bruce L. Mallory & Rebecca S. New (Eds.), *Diversity and developmentally appropriate practices: Challenges for early childhood education* (pp. 185–201). New York: Teachers College Press.

Ball, Stephen, Robert Hull, Martin Skelton, & Richard Tudor. 1984. The tyranny of the "devil's mill": Time and task at school. In Sara Delamont (Ed.), *Readings on interaction in the classroom* (pp. 41–57). London: Methuen.

Bandura, Albert. 1969. *Principles of behavior modification*. New York: Holt, Rinehart & Winston.

Bandura, Albert, & Richard Walters. 1963. *Social learning and personality development*. New York: General Learning.

Bateson, Gregory. 1971. The message: "This is play." In Robert E. Herron & Brian Sutton-Smith (Eds.), *Child's play* (pp. 261–266). New York: Wiley.

Bereiter, Carl, & Siegfried Engelmann. 1966. *Teaching the culturally disadvantaged child in the preschool*. Englewood Cliffs, NJ: Prentice-Hall.

Berlak, Ann, & Harold Berlak. 1981. *Dilemmas of schooling: Teaching and social change*. London and New York: Methuen.

Bowman, Barbara, & Frances Stott. 1994. Understanding development in a cultural context: The challenge for teachers. In Bruce L. Mallory & Rebecca S. New (Eds.), *Diversity and developmentally appropriate practices: Challenges for early childhood education* (pp. 119–133). New York: Teachers College Press.

Bredekamp, Sue (Ed.). 1987. Developmentally appropriate practice in early childhood programs serving children from birth through age 8. Washington, DC: National Association for the Education of Young Children.

Bredekamp, Sue, & Teresa Rosegrant (Eds.). 1992. *Reaching potentials: Appropriate curriculum and assessment for young children* (Vol. 1). Washington, DC: National Association for the Education of Young Children.

Bretherton, Inge. 1984. Representing the social world in symbolic play: Reality and fantasy. In Inge Bretherton (Ed.), *Symbolic play: The development of social understanding* (pp. 3–41). New York: Academic Press.

Britzman, Deborah. 1991. *Practice makes practice: A critical study of learning to teach*. Albany: State University of New York Press.

Bronfenbrenner, Urie. 1979. *The ecology of human development: Experiments by nature and design*. Cambridge, MA: Harvard University Press.

Brophy, Jere E., & Thomas Good. 1986. Teacher behavior and student achievement. In Merlin Wittrock (Ed.), *Handbook of research on teaching* (3rd ed.; pp. 570–602). New York: Macmillan.

Bruner, Jerome. 1986. *Actual minds, possible worlds*. Cambridge, MA: Harvard University Press.

Bruner, Jerome, Alison Jolly, & Kathy Sylva (Eds.). 1976. *Play: Its role in development and evolution*. New York: Penguin.

Burts, Diane, Craig Hart, Rosalind Charlesworth, & Lisa Kirk. 1990. A comparison of frequencies of stress behaviors observed in kindergarten children in classrooms with developmentally appropriate practices versus developmentally inappropriate instructional practices. *Early Childhood Research Quarterly, 5*(3), 407–420.

Caldwell, Bettye. 1984. What is quality child care? *Young Children, 39*(3), 3–8.

Christie, James F., & James E. Johnson. 1983. The role of play in social-intellectual development. *Review of Educational Research, 53*(1), 93–115.

Clandinin, Jean. 1986. *Classroom practice: Teacher images in action*. London: Falmer.

Clandinin, Jean. (March 1991) Workshop presentation, Mount Saint Vincent University, Halifax, Nova Scotia.

Comte, August. 1975. *A general view of positivism* (J. H. Bridges, Trans.). New York: Robert Speller and Sons. (Originally published 1830–1842)

Connelly, Michael, & Jean Clandinin. 1986. On narrative method, personal philosophy, and narrative unities in the story of teaching. *Journal of Research in Science Teaching, 23*(4), 293–310.

Connelly, Michael, & Clandinin, Jean. 1990. Stories of experience and narrative inquiry. *Educational Researcher, 19*(5), 2–14.

Corwin, Rebecca, George Hein, & Diane Levin. 1976. Weaving curriculum webs: The structure of nonlinear curriculum. *Childhood Education, 52*(5), 248–251.

Crain, William. 1992. *Theories of development: Concepts and applications* (3rd ed.). Englewood Cliffs, NJ: Prentice-Hall.

Dreikurs, Rudolph. 1964. *Children: The challenge*. New York: Hawthorn.

Duckworth, Eleanor. 1987. *"The having of wonderful ideas" and other essays on teaching and learning*. New York: Teachers College Press.

Dyson, Anne Haas. 1993. *Social worlds of children learning to write*. New York: Teachers College Press.

Edwards, Carolyn, Lella Gandini, & George Forman (Eds.). 1993. *The hundred languages of children: The Reggio Emilia approach to early childhood education*. Norwood, NJ: Ablex.

Eisner, Elliot. 1985. *The educational imagination* (2nd ed.). New York: Macmillan.

Elbaz, Freema. 1983. *Teacher thinking: A study of practical knowledge.* London: Croom Helm.

Erickson, Frederick. 1986. Qualitative methods in research on teaching. In Merlin Wittrock (Ed.), *Handbook of research on teaching* (3rd ed.; pp.119–161). New York: Macmillan.

Forman, George, & Fleet Hill. 1980. *Constructive play: Applying Piaget in the preschool.* Monterey, CA: Wadsworth.

Galinsky, Ellen. 1989. The staffing crisis. *Young Children, 44*(2), 3–5.

Gardner, Howard. 1978. *Developmental psychology.* Boston: Little, Brown.

Genishi, Celia, Anne Haas Dyson, & Rebekah Fassler. 1994. Language and diversity in early childhood: Whose voices are appropriate? In Bruce L. Mallory & Rebecca S. New (Eds.), *Diversity and developmentally appropriate practices: Challenges for early childhood education* (pp. 250–268). New York: Teachers College Press.

Gesell, Arnold. 1940. *The first five years of life: A guide to the development of the preschool child.* New York: Harper & Row.

Gesell, Arnold. 1971. *Studies in child development.* New York: Harper & Row. (Originally published 1948)

Ginsburg, Herbert, & Sylvia Opper. 1969. *Piaget's theory of intellectual development: An introduction.* Englewood Cliffs, NJ: Prentice-Hall.

Giroux, Henry, & Anthony Penna. 1981. Social education in the classroom: The dynamics of the hidden curriculum. In Henry Giroux, Anthony Penna, & William Pinar (Eds.), *Curriculum and instruction* (pp. 209–230). Berkeley, CA: McCutchan.

Giroux, Henry, Anthony Penna, & William Pinar (Eds.). 1981. *Curriculum and instruction.* Berkeley, CA: McCutchan.

Goffin, Stacy. 1989. Developing a research agenda for early childhood education: What can be learned from the research on teaching? *Early Childhood Research Quarterly, 4*(2), 187–204.

Grant, Carl, & Christine Sleeter. 1985. Who determines teacher work: The teacher, the organization, or both? *Teaching and Teacher Education, 1*(3), 209–220.

Greene, Maxine. 1988. Qualitative research and the uses of literature. In R. Sherman & R. Webb (Eds.), *Qualitative research in education: Focus and methods* (pp. 175–189). London: Falmer.

Halkes, Robert. 1988. Perspectives on teacher thinking: Comment on Clandinin and Connelly's study of the "personal" in studies of the personal. *The Journal of Curriculum Theorizing, 20*(2), 155–158.

Hatton, Elizabeth. 1987. Determinants of teacher work: Some causal complications. *Teaching and Teacher Education, 3*(1), 61–64.

Heath, Shirley Brice. 1983. *Ways with words: Language, life and work in communities and classrooms.* Cambridgeshire, England: Cambridge University Press.

Hendrick, Joanne. 1984. *The whole child* (2nd ed.). St. Louis: Mosby.

Hohmann, Mary, Bernard Banet, & David Weikart. 1978. *Young children in action.* Ypsilanti, MI: High/Scope Press.

Hunt, J. McVickers. 1964. Introduction to *The Montessori method* by Maria Montessori. New York: Schocken.

Illich, Ivan. 1983. *Gender*. London: Boyard.

Jackson, Philip. 1990. *Life in classrooms*. New York: Teachers College Press. (Originally published 1968)

Jones, Elizabeth. 1993. *Growing teachers: Partnerships in staff development*. Washington, DC: National Association for the Education of Young Children.

Jones, Elizabeth, & John Nimmo. 1994. *Emergent curriculum*. Washington, DC: National Association for the Education of Young Children.

Jones, Elizabeth, & Gretchen Reynolds. 1992. *The play's the thing: Teachers' roles in children's play*. New York: Teachers College Press.

Jorde-Bloom, Paula. 1986. Teacher job satisfaction: A framework for analysis. *Early Childhood Research Quarterly, 1*, 167–183.

Kamii, Constance, & Rheta DeVries. 1972. Piaget for education. In Mary C. Day & Ronald K. Parker (Eds.), *The preschool in action: Exploring early childhood programs* (pp. 363–420). Boston: Allyn & Bacon.

Kamii, Constance, & Rheta DeVries. 1993. *Physical knowledge in preschool education*. New York: Teachers College Press. (Originally published 1978)

Katz, Lillian, & Sylvia Chard. 1989. *Engaging children's minds: The project approach*. Norwood, NJ: Ablex.

Kessler, Shirley. 1991. Alternative perspectives on early childhood education. *Early Childhood Research Quarterly, 6*, 183–197.

Kramer, Rita. 1976. *Maria Montessori: A biography*. New York: Putnam.

Leach, Penelope. 1994. *Children first: What our society must do — and is not doing — for our children today*. New York: Knopf.

Levin, Diane. 1986. Weaving curriculum webs: Planning, guiding, and recording curriculum activities in the day care classroom. *Day Care and Early Education, 13*(4), 16–19.

Lillard, Paula Polk. 1980. *Children learning: A teacher's classroom diary*. New York: Schocken.

Lindberg, Lucille, & Rita Swedlow. 1976. *Early childhood education: A guide for observation and participation*. Boston: Allyn & Bacon.

Locke, John. 1964. *Some thoughts concerning education* (F. W. Garforth, Ed.). London: Heinemann. (Originally published 1693)

Lubeck, Sally. 1994. The politics of developmentally appropriate practice: Exploring issues of culture, class and curriculum. In Bruce L. Mallory & Rebecca S. New (Eds.), *Diversity and developmentally appropriate practices: Challenges for early childhood education* (pp. 17–43). New York: Teachers College Press.

Mallory, Bruce L., & Rebecca S. New. 1994. *Diversity and developmentally appropriate practices: Challenges for early childhood education*. New York: Teachers College Press.

Mandler, Jean Matter. 1984. *Stories, scripts and scenes: Aspects of schema theory*. Hillsdale, NJ: Erlbaum.

Montessori, Maria. 1964. *The Montessori method*. New York: Schocken.

NAEYC. Position statement on developmentally appropriate practice in programs for 4- and 5-year olds. 1986a. *Young Children, 41*(6), 20–29.

NAEYC. Position statement on developmentally appropriate practice in early childhood programs serving children from birth to age 8. 1986b. *Young Children, 41*(6), 3–19.

Nelson, Katherine. 1977. Cognitive development and the acquisition of concepts. In R. C. Anderson, R. Spiro, & W. Montague (Eds.), *Schooling and the acquisition of knowledge* (pp. 215–239). Hillsdale, NJ: Erlbaum.

New, Rebecca. 1993. Cultural variations on developmentally appropriate practice: Challenges to theory and practice. In Carolyn Edwards, Lella Gandini, & George Forman (Eds.), *The hundred languages of children: The Reggio Emilia approach to early childhood education* (pp. 215–231). Norwood, NJ: Ablex.

New, Rebecca. 1994. Culture, child development, and developmentally appropriate practices: Teachers as collaborative researchers. In Bruce L. Mallory & Rebecca S. New (Eds.), *Diversity and developmentally appropriate practices: Challenges for early childhood education* (pp. 65–83). New York: Teachers College Press.

Nias, Jennifer. 1986. Teacher socialization: The individual in the system. In *Sociology of the School*, a course offered by the School of Education, Deakin University's Open Campus Program. Victoria, Australia: Deakin University Press. ERIC microfilm.

Nova Scotia Department of Community Services. 1990. *Guidelines for operating a day care facility for children in Nova Scotia*. Halifax, Nova Scotia.

Paley, Vivian Gussin. 1985. *Superheroes in the doll corner*. Chicago: University of Chicago Press.

Paley, Vivian Gussin. 1990. *The boy who would be a helicopter*. Cambridge, MA: Harvard University Press.

Phillips, Carol Brunson. 1994. The movement of African American children through sociocultural contexts: A case of conflict resolution. In Bruce L. Mallory & Rebecca S. New (Eds.), *Diversity and developmentally appropriate practices: Challenges for early childhood education* (pp. 137–154). New York: Teachers College Press.

Phillips, Deborah, & Carollee Howes. 1987. Indicators of quality in child care: Review of research. In Deborah Phillips (Ed.), *Quality in child care: What does research tell us?* (pp. 1–19). Washington, DC: National Association for the Education of Young Children.

Piaget, Jean. 1954. *The construction of reality in the child* (Margaret Cook, Trans.). New York: Basic Books. (Originally published 1937)

Piaget, Jean. 1962. *Play, dreams and imitation* (C. Gattegno & F. M. Hodgson, Trans.). London: Routledge & Kegan Paul. (Originally published 1945)

Piaget, Jean, & Barbel Inhelder. 1969. *The psychology of the child*. London: Routledge & Kegan Paul.

Piaget, Jean. 1972. Some aspects of operations. In Maria Piers (Ed.), *Play and development: A symposium* (pp. 15–25). New York: Norton.

Polanyi, Michael. 1958. *Personal knowledge*. Chicago: University of Chicago Press.

Power, Edward J. 1991. *A legacy of learning: A history of Western education*. Albany: State University of New York Press.

Read, Katherine Baker, & J. Patterson. 1980. *Nursery school and kindergarten: Human relations and learning* (7th ed.). New York: Holt, Rinehart & Winston. (First edition published 1950)

Reifel, Stuart (Ed.). 1993. Perspectives on developmentally appropriate practice. *Advances in early education and day care* (vol. 5). Greenwich, CT: JAI Press.

Rogers, Carl. 1969. *Freedom to learn*. Columbus, OH: Merrill.

Rokeach, Milton. 1968. *Beliefs, attitudes and values: A theory of organization and change*. San Francisco: Jossey-Bass.

Rousseau, Jean-Jacques. 1979. *Émile or on education* (Alan Bloom, Trans.). New York: Basic Books. (Originally published 1764)

Rubin, Kenneth, & Deborah Pepler. 1980. The relationship of child's play to social-cognitive growth and development. In H. Foot, A. J. Chapman, & J. Smith (Eds.), *Friendship and social relationships in children* (pp. 209–233). London: Wiley.

Ruopp, Richard, Jeffrey Travers, Frederic Glantz, & Craig Coelen. 1979. *Children at the center: Final results of the national day care study*. Cambridge, MA: Abt Associates.

Sachs, Judith. 1987. The constitution of teachers' knowledge: A literature review. *Discourse, 7*(2), 92–98.

Schank, Roger, & Robert Abelson. 1977. *Scripts, plans, goals and understanding*. Hillsdale, NJ: Erlbaum.

Schön, Donald. 1983. *The reflective practitioner: How professionals think in action*. New York: Basic Books.

Schön, Donald. 1987. *Educating the reflective practitioner: Toward a new design for teaching and learning in the professions*. San Francisco: Jossey-Bass.

Schutz, Alfred. 1976. Recipe knowledge. In John Beck, Chris Jencks, Nell Keddie, & M. F. D. Young (Eds.), *Worlds apart: Readings for a sociology of education* (pp. 466–469). London: Collier Macmillan.

Schweinhart, Lawrence. May 1988. When the buck stops here: What it takes to run good early childhood programs. *Resource* (Newsletter of the High/Scope Research Foundation, Ypsilanti, MI) (pp. 1–6).

Seefeldt, Carol, & Nita Barbour. 1988. "They said I had to . . . :" Working with mandates. *Young Children, 43*(5), 4–8.

Sharp, Rachel, & Anthony Green. 1975. *Education and social control*. London: Routledge & Kegan Paul.

Shure, Myrna, & George Spivak. 1978. *Problem solving techniques in childrearing*. San Francisco: Jossey-Bass.

Smilansky, Sara. 1968. *The effects of sociodramatic play on disadvantaged preschool children*. New York: John Wiley.

Snider, Margaret. 1990. The effects of specialized education and job experience on early childhood teachers' knowledge of developmentally appropriate practice. *Early Childhood Research Quarterly*, 5, 69–78.

Stipek, Deborah. 1993. Is child-centered education really better? In Stuart Reifel (Ed.), *Perspectives in developmentally appropriate practice: Advances in early education and day care* Vol. 5. (pp. 29–52). Greenwich, CT: JAI Press.

Sutton-Smith, Brian. n. d. Play as a transformational set. *Leisure Today*. Undated reprint, approximately 1969.

Tyler, Ralph. 1968. *Basic principles of curriculum and instruction*. Chicago: University of Chicago Press. First published in 1950.

Vygotsky, Lev. 1978. *Mind in society: The development of higher psychological processes*. Cambridge, MA: Harvard University Press.

Whitebrook, M., Carollee Howes, & Deborah Phillips. 1990. Who cares? Child-care teachers and the quality of care in America (Executive Summary of the National Child Care Staffing Study). Oakland, CA: Child Care Employee Project.

Wien, Carol Anne. 1991. *Developmentally appropriate practice and the practical knowledge of day care teachers*. Unpublished doctoral dissertation, Dalhousie University, Halifax, Nova Scotia.

Williams, Leslie. 1994. Developmentally appropriate practice and cultural values: A case in point. In Bruce L. Mallory & Rebecca S. New (Eds.), *Diversity and developmentally appropriate practices: Challenges for early childhood education* (pp. 155–165). New York: Teachers College Press.

Yawkey, Thomas, & Anthony Pellegrini (Eds.). (1984). *Child's play and play therapy*. Lancaster, PA: Technomic.

Yinger, Robert. 1986. Examining thought in action: A theoretical and methodological critique of research on interactive teaching. *Teaching and Teacher Education*, 2(3), 163–282.

Index

About the Author

Carol Anne Wien is an assistant professor at York University in North York, Ontario; she has an M.A. and a Ph.D. in education from Dalhousie University, Halifax, Nova Scotia, and a B.A. from Queen's University, Kingston, Ontario. She has broad experience teaching curriculum to early childhood educators and coaching student teachers in field placements — as a lecturer in child study at Mount Saint Vincent University, in the Early Childhood Education Program, Halifax, and in several projects to train Mi'kmaq and Inuit women as day care workers. Previous to this she was a Montessori directress for 7 years, working first in Ithaca, New York; then London, Ontario; and Halifax, Nova Scotia. Her earliest work experience was as a high school teacher in Ontario.

She also writes adult short fiction; her stories have appeared in *The Pottersfield Portfolio* (1986, 1987, 1988, 1990), *Quarry Magazine* (Winter 1988, Summer Fiction Issue 1992), and Oberon Press's *Coming Attractions Series* (1988). Her first collection of stories, *Turtle Drum*, was published by Oberon Press in 1994.